DEVELOPING

CHARACTER
IN STUDENTS

A PRIMER

FOR TEACHERS, PARENTS, AND COMMUNITIES

Second Edition

Dr. Philip Fitch Vincent

Second edition, 1999; first edition, 1994

For information, contact:
Character Development Publishing
P.O. Box 9211
Chapel Hill NC 27515-9211
(919) 967-2110, fax (919) 967-2139
E-mail: respect96@aol.com
www.CharacterEducation.com

Cover design by Paul Turley
Text design by Dixon Smith & Janice Lewine
Text editing by Ginny Turner

ISBN 1-892056-04-6

$19.95

Quantity Purchases
Companies, schools, professional groups, clubs and other organizations may quality for special terms when ordering quantities of this title. For ordering information, contact the Customer Service Department of Character Development Publishing at the numbers listed above.

Dedication

This book is dedicated to my mother, Nellie Grace Fitch Vincent; to my father, Truby Adrian Vincent; and to my brother, David Adrian Vincent.

To my mother: Thank you for all your sacrifices in raising your boys and helping others throughout the community. You modeled the obligation we must hold toward others. I am honored to be your son.

To my father, who believed that World War II was about preserving democracy, who volunteered and fought as a marine on Iwo Jima, who participated in the occupation of Japan and then returned home without hate or anger toward anyone, who has lived a life of caring and love for all: I am honored to be your son.

To David, whom I always thought of as my twin: Although we are now separated by distance and cannot see each other as often as we would like, my love for you remains constant and growing. I am honored to be your brother.

My brother and I were raised by parents tempered by the Great Depression and World War II. We were loved and taught the importance of hard work and caring for others as the way to true happiness in life. My parents were right. You must give yourself to others to ever find yourself. David and I are passing this legacy to our children. In this way the wisdom of my parents will affect eternity.

Acknowledgments

I am pleased to recognize those around me who continue to offer encouragement and also challenge me to think and rethink my assumptions. What friends all of us in character education have in Thomas Lickona and Kevin Ryan! I'm grateful for our friendship. I have also discovered a great deal of powerful thought in the work of Gordon Vessels, Robert Nash, Edward DeRoche and Mary Williams, and Helen LeGette. You force me to think harder and deeper about the issues surrounding character education, which I deeply appreciate. Nancy Reed and Charlie Abourjilie are two of the hardest-working people in character education. I always leave your communities exhausted, but brimming with ideas.

My associates, Dixon Smith, Lisa Brumback, and Ginny Turner, are essential to Character Development Group. We're all striving to fulfill a mission of bringing the character education message to communities throughout the nation.

My wife, Cynthia, and daughter, Mary Kathryn, are the loves of my life. Without your love and support, none of this would be possible. I love you with all my heart for all time.

Contents

Chapter

CHARACTER IS SOMETHING EACH ONE OF US MUST build for himself out of the laws of God and nature, the examples of others, and—most of all—out of the trials and errors of daily life. Character is the total of thousands of small daily strivings to live up to the best that is in us. Character is the final decision to reject whatever is demeaning to oneself or to others with the confidence and honesty to choose the right.

—*General Arthur G. Trudeau*

Introduction

In *The De-moralization of Society* (1996), the noted thinker Gertrude Himmelfarb addressed the difference between values and virtues. I ask you to carefully consider this rather lengthy quote.

> It was in the 1880's that Friedrich Nietzsche began to speak of "values" in its present sense—not as a verb, meaning to value or esteem something; nor as a singular noun, meaning the measure of a thing (the economic value of money, labor, or property); but in the plural connoting the moral beliefs and attitudes of a society. Moreover, he used the word consciously, repeatedly, indeed insistently, to signify what he took to be the most profound event in human history. His "transvaluation of values" was to be the final, ultimate revolution, a revolution against both the classical virtues and the Judaic-Christian ones. The "death of God" would mean the death of morality and the death of truth—above all the truth of any morality. There would be no good and evil, no virtue and vice. There would be only "values." And having degraded virtues into values, Nietzsche proceeded to de-value and trans-value them, to create a new set of values for his "new man."...Values brought with it the assumptions that all moral ideas are subjective and relative, that they are mere customs and conventions, that they have a purely instrumental, utilitarian purpose, and that they are peculiar to specific individuals and societies.
>
> So long as morality was couched in the language of "virtue" it had a firm, resolute character. The older philosophers might argue about the source of virtues, the kinds and relative importance of virtues, the relation between moral and intellectual virtues or classical and religious ones, or the bearing of private virtues upon public ones. They might even "relativize" and "historicize" virtues by recognizing that different virtues characterized different peoples at different times and places. But for a particular people at a particular time, the word "virtue" carried with it a sense of gravity and authority, as "values" does not. (pp. 10-11)

Himmelfarb crystallizes in two paragraphs what I've been struggling to summarize over the last five years. What we are acting and reacting to is a society that has confused the virtues with values, preferences with standards. As educators, we know this from the values clarification movement. In values clarification, values were treated as virtues. All views were treated as equal. Standards were not needed. Values ruled. Preferences became the standards, and because there were no standards, all was accepted. The "new-man" of Nietzsche was being realized. This was further pushed in the 1980s and early 1990s in a fascination with self-esteem in the schools. Self-esteem was defined as feeling good. It was not treated as being good—for being good would demand standards or an appeal to virtue. Feeling good became an end in itself because we were reluctant to establish standards of behavior for both students and teachers.

However, in the early- to mid-'90s, teachers, parents, and communities began to realize that values clarification and the focus on self-esteem weren't creating the society they envisioned for themselves and their children. Many people began to realize there were standards that should be taught in schools and lived out in society. Teachers and parents from various political and social groups began to realize and discuss that feeling good is not the same as being good and that perhaps we should model and have children practice the habits that lead to knowing, loving, and doing the good. Perhaps we should reconsider the role of character education in the school and the community.

Himmelfarb's presentation of Nietzsche's transformation of virtues into values represented the precursor of the rise of values clarification and the self-esteem movement in American schools. Ryan and Bohlin present its antithesis, the recognition that good-willed people can come to an agreement on certain moral standards and virtues that should be modeled and taught to all children. Thus the re-emergence of character education in the 1990s within American schools and communities.

I am honored to be a small part of this effort. Traveling around the country has given me a wonderful appreciation of its teachers, families, and communities. People are sitting down and talking to each other. They are determining the character traits that children need to know and that they need to model. Communities around the country are deciding that character education is as important as their schools' focus on academics.

I've seen this in Graham County, North Carolina, where a small, isolated mountain community has developed a wonderful character education program from pre-K through 12th grade. As the teachers modeled what was expected, the children followed right along. Now the teachers and students serve each other and others in the community throughout the year.

I've seen the impact of character education in Chattanooga (Hamilton County), Tennessee. This wonderful city completed a physical renewal that has been recognized and modeled by other forward-thinking civic leaders around the world. Now the Chattanooga schools are focusing on their moral renewal. With efforts in the community and in the schools, they are uniting to insure that all their citizens model and teach to children the importance of good character. Next year a book will be published documenting the results of their efforts.

I've seen individuals teachers and principals leading the efforts in their schools. For these individuals, character education is a return to the true calling of education—to help children become smarter and better. It is because of this desire to develop the minds and hearts of children that the best teachers choose education as their life's work. The resurgence of character education validates their efforts.

Ultimately I've learned far more from the teachers, administrators, and citizens of communities throughout the nation than I have ever taught them. From them, I have become a conduit, sharing their insights and enthusiasm with other like-minded souls throughout the country. I cannot personally thank all of you, but I am grateful for our time together. My life is far richer because of you.

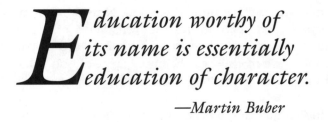

Education worthy of its name is essentially education of character.

—*Martin Buber*

Chapter 1

The Need for Character Education

Ms. Jackson is a secondary-level history teacher known for being very demanding. Her students don't just read the textbook and answer the chapter questions. They spend library time researching primary sources, they read various voices of the historical era reflected in literature, and they discuss ideas in seminars. But her "bad" reputation comes more from her high expectations for student behavior. Ms. Jackson models and expects civility in her classroom at all times

She began the year by asking her students what went into a class climate that was respectful, responsible, and caring. She told them that once they came to agreement on what their class should feel like, she expected that all students would behave in a way to make it feel like that. She herself models the positive character traits she expects her students to demonstrate. She's always on time, always prepared, always courteous. She readily apologizes when she is in error and expects sincere apologies from students when they are wrong. Every day she uses Hal Urban's beginning-of-class procedure, asking students to share any good news and thanking those students who have been especially helpful. She holds students accountable for their assignments and doesn't accept many excuses. She requires them to honor their word, even when it causes them to feel angry toward her. If problems arise in class, she will, if appropriate, attempt to solve them as a community.

Ms. Jackson is a very demanding teacher—but her students always score very well on standardized tests, and they like to come back to tell her about their achievements in other grades.

Mr. Williams is an elementary-level teacher. At the beginning of each school year, he spends time asking his students to describe what being respectful, responsible, and caring toward each other looks and sounds like to them. They take time to draw pictures of themselves acting this way, which he mounts on poster paper. He explains that this is how he expects them to act in his room, and their own ideas become the procedures or practices of the class.

Each day during the first week of school, he has the students practice being respectful, responsible, and caring in the classroom and throughout the school environment. They notice and praise children who demonstrate respect, responsibility, and caring especially well. Mr. Williams spends this time during the first week of school to establish good habits in the students, which he expects to continue throughout the school year.

Mr. Williams always holds a morning meeting to discuss the forthcoming day. Students are encouraged to share particular achievements or unusual activities and to thank others for showing good character. He uses opportunities that come up during reading activities to discuss issues of appropriate actions. He feels his classroom is a community, and he teaches his children to demonstrate inclusion and civility toward all. He involves them in helping solve many problems that arise in the classroom. Though Mr. Williams has spent his first class week discussing right behavior, he never has trouble completing the curriculum. He is immensely popular with the students, as well as with the parents of his children.

Both Ms. Jackson and Mr. Williams feel they'd be remiss as educators if they didn't work to help shape their students' character as well as their intellect. Indeed, both of these educators feel that character development is as important as academic achievement.

When I wrote the first edition of this book in 1994, I sensed that many educators were not as intent on character development as Ms. Jackson and Mr. Williams. Many teachers were reluctant to adopt the mission of working within the school environment, as well as working with parents and communities, in helping to shape the character of their students. Five years ago, they seemed averse to, or at the least confused about, how they could assume the role of a "moral compass" in the lives of children in their classrooms.

Some didn't regard it as important to model, instruct, practice, and talk with students to help them develop good habits and insights into the understanding of traits such as honesty, respect, and truthfulness. Many came out and said that character education was the responsibility of parents and not an area schools in which should be involved. Other educators preferred to follow the lead of the French philosopher Jean-Jacques Rousseau and allow children to figure out morality on their own. Still others felt that schools should be involved only in the academic world, and thus any discussion or teaching of virtues such as respect, responsibility, kindness, or caring would violate the mission of the school.

All these reasons to ignore or limit the importance of character education in schools have historical precedents in American education, starting in the 1940s and gaining a full head of steam by the 1960s and '70s. Luckily for our children and our careers as educators, this mind-set is rapidly changing. As I write this, I am proud to say that *whether* character education should be a part of the curriculum in our schools is no longer the issue—we have now moved to determining *what* we should be doing to facilitate the character development of our students. Educators are returning to the belief that one of their obligations is to be the children's "parents away from the home" and that this entails both their academic and moral education.

The school's role in this effort of assisting parents and communities in the character education of children is getting the attention of businesses and community leaders throughout the country. For example, Sanford McDonnell, Chairman Emeritus of McDonnell/Douglas Aerospace Corporation, has been a champion of schools, working hard to help develop the character of youth. He works with and speaks to communities throughout the nation regarding the importance of character education in the schools. In two books—*The Spirit of Community: The Reinvention of American Society* (1994) and *The New Golden Rule: Community and Morality in a New Democratic Society* (1997)—and in his work at the Communitarian Network in Washington, D.C., Amitai Etzioni addresses the important role that schools and communities must play in helping develop the moral character of our youth. It is as if we as a nation are finally acknowledging Kevin Ryan's statement that character education represents schools' oldest mission. In America, there is a great deal of precedent concerning the role of character education in America's public schools.

No single writer has illustrated the character development mission of the public schools more clearly than B. Edward McClellan, professor of education and American studies at Indiana University. In his excellent work, *Schools and the Shaping of Character: Moral Education in America, 1607-Present* (1992), he outlines the role public schools have played in helping shape the character of their students. (He also talks about the role of private and public universities in the shaping of character, but we will focus just on the public schools.) Although his work is far too extensive to discuss at great length in this book, I highlight below some of his historical narrative as well as some curricular examples to illustrate how character education has been implemented in the public schools.

1600s—Recognizing the moral training of children began in the home, agencies such as schools, churches, and apprenticeships were enlisted to continue moral training with a distinct emphasis on the tenets of the Christian faith. The intensive training began early. Religion was critical in this approach, with the expected recitations of the basic doctrines of Christian faith. This focus was echoed in Massachusetts schools with the passage of an enactment called the "Ould Deluder Satan" law of 1647, which required schoolmasters in towns of 50 households and schools in those of 100 households or more. The intent of the schools was to prepare some children for higher education to insure the colony educated leaders capable of continuing and preserving the Christian values of the new land.

1700s—As the nation developed along the Atlantic coast, the community played an increasing role in the development of character. Moral education was received through the family, church, and apprenticeships, but could also be learned through communities, and elders within the community. With this effort, society's values and Christian virtues could be inculcated in its youth. Moral education was viewed as a long-term process. One could learn good character throughout one's life. This more relaxed standard and teaching format were not recognized by all, especially those with a more evangelical bent, who continued to employ a rigorous approach to child rearing and moral instruction. Still, the more moderate approach was very influential in society as a whole.

1800s—Moral education was being formalized and was, in some ways, returning to the approach of character development found in the 1600s through the early 1700s. This was a rationale for a more intensive/direct approach. As the nation moved westward, there was a feeling that time was of the essence. There would no longer be the luxury of the long apprenticeship into the mores of a community. The elders and strong communities that had played such an important role in character development of their citizens were no longer available for a growing, mobile population. People were on the move from one place to another. Moral education would receive less emphasis within the community and would demand a systematic effort on the part of schools and parents. McClellan notes:

> As Americans contemplated the prospect of sending their children into these dangerous worlds [cities and the frontier], they gave to moral education an urgency it had often lacked in the eighteenth century. They also gave it a quality of definition and systematization it had never had in the colonial period. Increasingly children acquired their values in common ways, through agencies assigned special responsibility for their education. (p. 19)

Schools became an "agency" where character development was considered a vital mission. Women began to replace men as the school educators. Women who had strong moral character were sought out since they were considered experts in moral training based on their work in the home. This was considered critically important since students would learn best from one who exhibited the virtues. The aims of the classroom were to have an orderly environment, to cultivate a love of virtue, and to develop good habits that children would carry outside the classroom. The textbooks emphasized morality, self-restraint, and good citizenship, utilizing Protestant morality and 19th–century goals of good citizenship, which included honesty, courage, morality, and the character traits needed to be a productive citizen in a changing world. The focus was on developing the morality of the citizen for both the private and public life.

McClellan, citing Horace Mann, notes that the goal of public school moral education was to

> build up a partition wall—a barrier—so thick and high between the principles of right and wrong in the minds of men that the future citizens will not overleap or break through it. A truly conscientious man, whatever may be his desire, his temptation, his appetite, the moment he approaches the boundary line which separates right from wrong, beholds an obstruction—a barrier—more impassable than a Chinese wall. He could sooner leap the ocean than transgress it. (pp. 26-27)

One can find examples of how Mann's vision was organized in the textbooks used to inculcate values in children. In 1848, a moral education manual by A. Hall was published. The following is taken from the title page and table of contents of this manual:

A MANUAL OF MORALS FOR COMMON SCHOOLS
ADAPTED ALSO TO THE USE OF FAMILIES.

Contents

It's clear just from this table of contents that the school was expected to play a vital role in the formation and development of a child's values. The popular McGuffey's Readers followed the same general pattern. By continually being exposed to writings and ideas that emphasized the importance of developing good character, students would learn the character traits needed to be successful and moral individuals. It was hoped that students would mimic what they had read. Consider the following selections taken from the McGuffey's *Fifth Eclectic Reader* (1920 ed.):

> THE education, moral and intellectual, of every individual, must be chiefly his own work. Rely upon it that the ancients were right; both in morals and intellect we give the final shape to our characters, and thus become, emphatically, the architects of our own fortune....And of this be assured, I speak from observation a certain truth: THERE IS NO EXCELLENCE WITHOUT GREAT LABOR. It is the fiat of fate, from which no power of genius can absolve you. (William Wirt [1772–1834]) (pp. 230–231)

> NO one has a temper naturally so good, that it does not need attention and cultivation, and no one has a temper so bad, but that, by proper culture, it may become pleasant. One of the best disciplined tempers ever seen, was that of a gentleman who was naturally quick, irritable, rash, and violent; but, by having the care of the sick, and especially of deranged people, he so completely mastered himself that he was never known to be thrown off his guard....There is no misery so constant, so distressing, and so intolerable to others, as that of having a disposition which is your master, and which is continually fretting itself. (John Todd, D.D. [1800–1873]) (p. 204)

> RELIGION is a social concern; for it operates powerfully on society, contributing in various ways to its stability and prosperity. Religion is not merely a private affair; the community is deeply interested in its diffusion; for it is the best support of the virtues and principles on which the social order rests. (William Ellery Channing [1780–1842]) (p. 264)

Notice the infusion of religion in Hall's and McGuffey's work in relation to the obligations that an individual had toward society. It was felt that the morality of the citizenry rather than the structure of government would determine the success of individuals and the nation.

McClellan notes, "The nineteenth-century tendency to place personal moral conduct at the core of their hope for social stability and political liberty gave to the common school a significance it had never had before." (p. 27)

1900s–present By the late 1800s and the early 1900s, focused moral education was receiving less attention in the schools due to increasing requirements on schools to teach more intensively social, academic, and vocational skills, which were increasingly in demand within an economically and industrially developing nation. To be successful, one needed more than character. One also needed "skills, efficiency and social competence." (McClellan, p. 53). Educators began to question whether moral readings and classroom teachers who led, encouraged and urged their students to be good would be sufficient to meet the needs of a changing, industrial, scientifically based society. Character development focus moved from individual accountability to group involvement. It became more activity-based. The popularity of 4–H and boy and girl scouting increased. High school clubs to do good works within a community were organized. In schools, citizenship grades on report cards were regularly given. Another change concerned the development of moral codes that addressed the obligations of a good citizenry without the appeal to religious dictates. The "progressives," under the leadership of John Dewey, attempted to apply science and reason to the issues and problems of the day. No longer was an appeal to religious principles or sensitivities needed. Indeed, the progressives focused more on social and political issues than individual morality. McClellan notes:

> By emphasizing critical thinking, for example, progressives gave students a basis for questioning arbitrary authority, for abandoning outmoded traditions, and for meeting the novel challenges of a world in flux. By emphasizing ethical flexibility and sensitivity to situation, they prepared them to deal with the varying demands of a highly segmented society in which different arenas called for different moral responses. By teaching them to judge actions by social consequence, they gave them a new, purely secular, standard by which to make moral decisions. (p. 65)

Yet, as McClellan notes, progressivism was not without serious consequences. "By denigrating tradition, weakening the authority of adults, and giving new legitimacy to peer influence, progressivism left students vulnerable to the tyranny of both the immediate group and the present moment." (p. 68) Despite concerns about the progressives and other more traditional methods of character education, efforts in shaping the character of youth continued. Moral education was still considered a part of the curriculum although it did not have the sharpened approach of the 19th century and reflected a variety of approaches. Many schools organized service clubs and continued a strong teacher-led, literature-based focus on the importance of developing a good character. Social studies education increased in popularity and importance. By the 1940s and '50s, the slow but steady retreat of moral education was being facilitated by the continuing demands of greater cognitive development and academic education of students. There was no deliberate intent to throw moral education out of the curriculum—educators simply felt there was not enough time for character education since students needed more time to master greater academic demands.

By the 1960s and '70s, moral education was in full retreat. The Vietnam war and other cultural upheavals had Americans reeling. Cultural relativism was leading the way as Americans questioned whether there could be common ground or even common standards concerning what was good or right conduct for citizens. Educators claimed, "If we can't come to an agreement on what good character is, then perhaps we should leave it out." To avoid controversy and unpleasantness, it was easier and perhaps "safer" for public school teachers to abdicate the instruction of values to parents and church.

Still, many parents and educators had a desire to do something about values. One such attempt was the values clarification approach of the 1960s and '70s, which emphasized allowing each student to clarify what he or she felt without judgment against objective or consistent standards. The teacher would act as the "supporter," not a moral compass in the life of children. Morality and character were based on personal preferences, with no attempt to lead children toward community expectations of honesty, responsibility, or other aspects of good character.

Another approach was the cognitive/moral developmental approach first advocated by Lawrence Kohlberg. To Kohlberg, there were stages of moral development, with each successive stage reflecting a higher level of moral reasoning of an individual. The higher the stage, supposedly the better one would act concerning moral issues.

Some of his students and disciples, including this author, devised practices to facilitate moral reasoning in students. Ultimately the values clarification and the cognitive/moral developmental approach left schools with few ideas to help shape the moral character of their students. I'll address both of these approaches more in the next chapter.

In conclusion, McClellan's historical research clearly illustrates that moral education played an important role in American education from the earliest schools. The slow decline in moral education began in the 1940s and '50s with a greater emphasis placed on academics. By the '60s and '70s, moral education in the schools was in complete retreat. However, in the '90s, moral or character education is gaining renewed interest.

The Reawakening Interest in Character Education

Peter Senge, in his book *The Fifth Discipline: The Art and Practice of the Learning Organization* (1991), relates a Sufi tale that is especially relevant for the educational community.

> Once there was a rug merchant who saw that his most beautiful carpet had a large bump in its center. He stepped on the bump to flatten it out—and succeeded. But the bump reappeared in a new spot not far away. He jumped on the bump again, and it disappeared—for a moment, until it emerged once more in a new place. Again and again he jumped, scuffing and mangling the rug in his frustration; until finally he lifted one corner of the carpet and an angry snake slithered out. (p. 57)

In recent years, professional educators have continually stepped on the bumps in the rug rather than look under the rug to identify the real problems and thereby formulate viable solutions. In this way educators are much like everyone else. Looking under the rug is difficult and troublesome, but if we step on the bumps only when the problems appear, we merely transfer the problems to another area. We cannot solve the problems until we begin to look under the rug.

The problems that cause the bumps in the rug for education are the same ones that cause the bumps in society. Schools do not exist apart from society; they mirror it. Many of our schools' problems reflect deep, pervasive, personal, and societal ills such as drug and alcohol abuse, child abuse, neglect, poverty, unemployment, and violence. In

1998, four middle school children and a teacher in Jonesboro, Arkansas, were murdered by two classmates. Other slayings of students by students occurred in Kentucky, Oregon, New Jersey, and—worst of all— Littleton, Colorado. In November 1998, several high school students in Burlington, Wisconsin, were charged with planning a shooting assault at their school, with the principal being a chief target. Luckily, some- one alerted the authorities and the boys were arrested.

On January 2, 1999, the Justice Department reported that the nation's murder rate fell in 1997 to a level last seen in 1957. The rate was 6.8 murders per 100,000 people, down from a high of 10.2 in 1980. The incidents of firearms killings by those 25 years old and older plummeted by roughly half to about 5,000 between 1980 and 1997. That's the good news. Gun killings by those age 18-24 **increased** from about 5,000 in 1980 to more than 7,500 in 1997. And these statistics do not include those younger than 18! Imagine 30 years ago thinking about children killing others. Yet today schools must consider this. Schools around the country are installing metal detectors to at least try to keep guns and knives out of the school. A new vocational high school in Dallas, Texas, spent more than $3 million on security concerns.

In 1997 the State of North Carolina released a report on juvenile crime from 1987 to 1996. During a time when adult crime was decreasing, adolescent crime increased tremendously. Violent crimes were up 172%. Weapons law violations were up 482%. Drug violations were up 523%. All arrests for juveniles were up 105%. It's likely that this pattern is similar in other states.

Less physically dangerous, but equally disturbing, many educa- tors are having to address a general lack of civility in schools. A report released by the Educational Testing Service in 1998 compared the per- centage of public school principals reporting various discipline issues as being serious or moderate problems in their high schools in the school years 1990-91 and 1996–97. The researcher noted that "there were several significant differences between 1991 and 1997. In 1997, more principals reported that student tardiness, absenteeism, class-cutting, drug use, sale of drugs on school grounds, and verbal abuse of teachers were serious or moderate problems." (p. 31)

I travel extensively and talk to teachers all over the country. When I ask experienced teachers if it's easier or harder to teach now than 20 years ago, they invariably reply that it's more difficult to teach because of the moral issues they are encountering. An educational communication for *Who's Who Among America's Teachers* was reported in *USA Today* on September 9, 1997. It reported these percentages of veteran teachers (79% have taught more than 10 years) said students had declined in the following ways over their teaching careers:

Less respectful of authority	81%
Less ethical/moral	73%
Less responsible	65%
More self-centered	60%

What we have to realize is that our children have learned this. Children come into this world with a clean slate. As William Damon has noted, they come into the world with the necessary "wiring" to be good or bad. We, as adults, provide the activating moral current. Whatever the youth have learned, they have learned from adults, whether in the home, community, or through the popular media. Let us consider the popular media.

First, let me state that I don't believe that just watching violence on TV will make a child violent. I believe that most children can separate violence or disturbing images or ideas on TV from real life. However, I'm concerned when far too many children have little to counter what they see and hear on television. I'm concerned when parents don't declare certain television programs off limits for their children or don't watch the programs with them and discuss how what they see and hear might differ from their own values of civility or decency. Unfortunately, there is no such thing as family TV hour today. With rampant syndication, programs with mature themes and dialogue that originally ran after 9 pm are regularly being shown as reruns between 5 and 7:30 pm—just when many parents are wearily re-entering family life from their workday. As a parent, I have to censor what my child will watch on TV the entire day. Programming at any time of day may challenge your basic virtues. Where are Claire and Cliff Huxtable? Where is Andy or Aunt Bee? Where are the Waltons? They are few and far between.

In 1997, WB network introduced "Dawson's Creek," a program aimed at young teenagers. In the first episode, one of the actors found his mother having an illicit affair; the second had the female lead admitting she'd been sleeping around since she was 12; and in the third, a teenage boy lost his virginity to his teacher, who by the fourth episode was trying to work through this event herself as an adult! This is a very popular program, as is "South Park," a cartoon about foul-talking children and their friend, a talking pile of feces. "The Jerry Springer Show" features seriously dysfunctional people in violent and foul-mouthed encounters in front of a cheering audience. Is this what you want your children to see?

What about music? Take the time to listen to the lyrics of Marilyn Manson or some rappers such as Tupac Shakur. Would you want your son to treat women the way these individuals advocate? Some rock lyrics will horrify you.

How many of you have seen what is readily available on the Internet? Fully 25% of the "hits" on Web pages are for pornography. The great American educator and philosopher John Dewey, in his work *School and Society* (1910), stated, "What the best and wisest parent wants for his own child, that must the community want for all of its children." Clearly we need Claire and Cliff Huxtable more than we need "Dawson's Creek." We must help our children learn to sift through the popular culture and judge it based on moral virtues, not on what is popular.

There is much that the "best and wisest" parents would recommend to other parents and to schools. Some would recommend trying to live out our virtues and act as models to our children. Others would recommend that we intentionally teach these virtues to our children in the home, community, and school. What we must now do is begin addressing this issue. William Kilpatrick, in his fine book *Why Johnny Can't Tell Right from Wrong* (1992), addresses the issue with clarity and power.

> The core problem facing our schools is a moral one. All other problems derive from it, and, as a result, no attempt at school reform is likely to succeed unless character education is put at the top of the agenda. If students don't learn self-discipline and respect for others, they will continue to exploit each other sexually no matter how many health clinics and condom-distribution plans are created. If they don't learn habits of courage and justice, curriculums designed to improve their self-esteem won't stop the epidemic of extortion, bullying and violence; neither will courses designed to make them more sensitive to diversity. Even academic reform depends on putting character first (p. 225).

But how might a teacher, with the understanding that her efforts must work to supplement those in the home and community, help mold and develop good character in her students? First, we must recognize that not all character is taught. Much of it is caught—learned by watching the actions of adults. Second, there are virtues that are not controversial and can be taught within a school. I have yet to meet a parent who didn't want school to assist children in becoming respectful, caring, and responsible for their actions. I have yet to meet a parent who didn't want kindness, honesty, and courage modeled at school and taught to children. Or one who didn't want someone like Ms. Jackson or Mr. Williams, whom we met at the beginning of this chapter, teaching his or her child. In his book *Educating for Character* (1991), Thomas Lickona describes the teaching of respect and responsibility as reflecting the public school's moral agenda: "Respect and responsibility are the 'fourth and fifth R's' that schools not only may but also must teach if they are to develop ethically literate persons who can take their place as responsible citizens of society." (p. 43)

There are many virtues or traits most people would like to possess and have their children develop. Several authors have created lists.

Thomas Lickona, in addition to respect and responsibility, nominated:

FAIRNESS	TOLERANCE	PRUDENCE
SELF-DISCIPLINE	HELPFULNESS	COMPASSION
COOPERATION	COURAGE	HONESTY
HOST OF DEMOCRATIC VALUES		(p. 45)

Steven Covey (1989) recognized:

INTEGRITY	TEMPERANCE	SIMPLICITY
HUMILITY	JUSTICE	FIDELITY
COURAGE	INDUSTRY	PATIENCE
MODESTY	THE GOLDEN RULE	(p. 18)

The National School Boards Association recognized the following values as important to a "democratic and humane society:"

ALTRUISM	LOYALTY	COMPASSION
OBEDIENCE	COURAGE	PUNCTUALITY
COURTESY	GENEROSITY	TOLERANCE
RESPONSIBILITY	HONESTY	SELF-DISCIPLINE
INDUSTRIOUSNESS	SELF-RESPECT	INTEGRITY
RESPECT FOR AUTHORITY		(Scotter et al., 1991, 95)

In July 1992, the Josephson Institute of Ethics brought together educators and youth leaders to discuss how to advance character education. The participants in the conference came up with six values they called "pillars" of character. The six pillars and their support values are listed below:

TRUSTWORTHINESS honesty, integrity, promise-keeping, loyalty

RESPECT .... autonomy, privacy, dignity, courtesy, tolerance, acceptance

RESPONSIBILITY .... accountability, pursuit of excellence

CARING .... compassion, consideration, giving, sharing, kindness, loving

FAIRNESS .... procedural fairness, impartiality, consistency, equality, equity, due process

CITIZENSHIP .... law-abiding, community service, protection of environment   (Josephson, p. 80)

Finally, Edward Wynne and Kevin Ryan, in their book, *Reclaiming Our Schools, Second Edition* (1997), recognize eight ethical ideals or values which could be considered the proper goals of humanity. The first four ideas and definitions are taken from the ancient Greeks:

PRUDENCE .... is the habit of acting with discretion and deliberation.

JUSTICE .... is the quality of being righteous and fair.

TEMPERANCE .... is the state of being self-restrained in conduct, being under one's own control.

FORTITUDE .... is the capacity to withstand misfortune with bravery.

The next three moral ideals are found within many world religions.

FAITH has two meanings. The original is the capacity to put trust and reliance in God and the confidence that comes from that trust. Faith can also mean the trust and confidence we put in another person or institution.

HOPE is the habit of desiring the good with at least a slight expectation of obtaining it, or the belief that it is indeed obtainable. It is confidence in the future.

CHARITY is a habit of the heart, a disposition to think favorably of other people. Finally there is a trait that can be considered both a philosophical and religious concept.

DUTY is a disposition to be loyal to those, both above us and below us, to whom we have an obligation. It involves our sense of responsibility to something outside ourselves. (pp. 140-141)

Religious traditions have always offered guidelines to help individuals recognize and develop the traits required of good character. Within the intellectual traditions of Judaism, Christianity, and Islam we find similar teachings:

You shall not take vengeance, nor bear any grudge against the children of your people, but you shall love your neighbor as yourself: I am the Lord. (Leviticus 19:16)

But I say to you, love your enemies, bless those who curse you, do good to those who hate you, and pray for those who spitefully use you and persecute you. (Matthew 5:44)

Worship Allah and associate naught with Him, and conduct yourselves with beneficence towards parents, and toward kindred, and orphans, and the needy, and toward the neighbor, that is of the kindred, and the neighbor that is a stranger, and the companions by your side, and the wayfarer and those who work for you. (Koran 4:37–38)

Help one another in righteousness and virtue; but help not one another in sin and transgression. (Koran 5:3)

The teachings of Buddha and Confucius also offer many guides for a virtuous life. From Buddhism we recognize writings on the importance and power of love, which are recapitulated in the Judeo-Christian tradition:

Hatred does not cease by hatred;
Hatred ceases only by love.
This is an eternal law. (Dhammapada 1960, 5)

Let a man overcome hatred by kindness, evil by goodness, greed by generosity, and lies by telling the truth. (Dhammapada 1960, 223)

The Analects of Confucius (1993) records various conversations between Confucius and his disciples. One conversation concerns how a person could obtain Zen, or perfect virtue. Notice how the advice parallels the teaching of Jesus regarding how we should treat others.

> Zigong asked: "Is there a single word such that one could practice it throughout one's life?" The Master said: "Reciprocity, perhaps? Do not inflict on others what yourself would not wish done to you." (15.24)

These teachings, as well as many others from various religious and ethical traditions, provide guidelines to help us live better lives with respect to others. And isn't the act of treating others with respect an important part of maintaining a civil society? I may disagree with you on a particular issue, but how I treat you as a person should not be tied to your point of view. I consider this a basic courtesy. A question we must consider is whether basic courtesies and appropriate behaviors, which help formulate a person of character, are being taught and modeled as well as they should be in society today.

Are we teaching that the needs of others may require a sacrifice on our part? Based on my experiences, I believe that schools, as well as society, have on occasion failed to model and teach what it means to be respectful and practice responsibility toward others. As a society, we are often neglecting basic courtesies and appropriate behaviors that make up good character. We have forgotten that many times the needs of others require a sacrifice on our part. In schools as well as in society, we have neglected to teach our students and our children to be respectful and to practice responsibility toward others. We have far too often failed to model and instruct children in the importance of caring. If we can agree on some values we wish our students to have, and if we believe these values are found in people we recognize as having good character, we need to formulate a plan for developing these values in our students. To be successful, we must recognize that a crucial role of schools is to facilitate the development of character and thereby develop an educational strategy to remove our gridlock on the teaching of positive virtues in students.

Most children or students are not disrespectful or irresponsible. Parents, communities, and schools continue to teach and model virtues such as respect, responsibility, and caring. But as an educator for more than 20 years, I am seeing these characteristics less and less often, especially if schools have not implemented character education programs. More students and their elders appear to be far more oriented to having their own needs met, however impulsive or self-centered their needs may be. Working with and helping others, as well as taking responsibility for one's actions, seem to be undesirable choices for many.

In a 1996 survey involving 6,000 high school students, Michael Josephson of the Josephson Institute of Ethics reported that 87% of the students believed that honesty was the best policy. Yet 65% admitted they had cheated on an exam in the previous year. Some 73% said they had lied to their parents more than once in the previous year. In addition, 42% of the males and 31% of the females admitted they had stolen something from a store during the previous 12 months; 29% said they had stolen something from a parent. Unfortunately, the 1998 Josephson survey indicated little had changed. When I ask teachers around the country to complete the statement: "It's all right to steal as long as…," I always hear in unison, "you don't get caught!" Why would I hear this throughout the country?

Perhaps we need to have adults as well as children practice what they preach. If you value caring, then practice caring. If you value honesty, then practice honesty. We must also acknowledge that the impact of this is limited. In the case of many students, home life is dismal at best. For many others, home life seems acceptable, but something is still missing. Perhaps the child has grown up with parents whose needs have taken precedence over the child's. Maybe there has been little emphasis on caring, both within the family and community. Perhaps no one has made the little sacrifices that develop a good family environment. These self-centered children—rather than outward-looking, family-oriented, community-oriented children—could eventually pose a serious threat to society and themselves. When one doesn't feel a part of a family, school, or community, one has little to gain by participating in them. If one is not cared about or hasn't learned to care for others, then one has little to gain by participating in the family, school, or community.

The importance of teaching people to care cannot be overstated. Samuel and Pearl Oliner interviewed many persons who chose either to help or not help rescue Jews during World War II. The authors were looking for personality characteristics of individuals who would risk their own lives to save others. In their book, *The Altruistic Personality:*

Rescuers of Jews in Nazi Europe (1988), the authors explain that "close family relationships in which parents model caring behavior and communicate caring values" (p. 249) contributed to the development of caring and compassionate persons who chose to help rescue Jews even though their own lives were in danger. Although the Oliners' research indicated the importance of the home and community, the school environment should also be a setting where the practice and discussion of the importance of good character and the obligations we have towards others must occur.

The remainder of this book will focus on formulating a plan to help educators create schools where developing character is as important as academics. We're aiming to restore the balance that has reflected the historic mission of America's schools.

Chapter 2

Teaching for Character Development

Values clarification and cognitive moral education are two methods that were utilized fairly extensively through the 1960s-1980s. I am discussing these methods because of their influence on thinking about character or moral education. Both strategies are generally less influential now than in the past, but it behooves us to examine them and consider how their implications are still affecting education in the United States. We should also recognize that both values clarification and cognitive moral education have some strengths, but neither is adequate to develop good character in youth. To analyze the deficiencies of these approaches, let us begin with the older and more popular of the two methods.

Values Clarification

Starting in the mid-1960s and gaining strength well into the 1970s, the values clarification philosophy took hold in schools throughout the United States. The cultivation of objective standards of behavior, as well as the development of consistent habits such as respect and responsibility, was de-emphasized in school, community, and, in some cases, the home. Careful analysis and the development of rational thought were neglected in favor of "feeling good" and knowing how one feels about an issue. In a school using values clarification, educators no longer had to consider an objective or moral standard such as the Western intellectual tradition or religious-based ethical pronouncements. The presumption was that since everyone has values, everyone—

and every child—knows what is moral or at least what is moral for him or her! Yet values represent preferences and choices. Virtues represent standards to assess actions or pronouncements. Eliminate virtue and moral choices become subjective—requiring only statement or clarification—thus values clarification.

One of the most widely used methods in values education, values clarification was first formulated by Louis Raths, Merrill Harmin, and Sidney Simon in *Values and Teaching* (1966) and followed up with Simon, Leland Howe, and Howard Kirshenbaum's *Values Clarification* (1972). The latter, an activities book, sold more than 600,000 copies. It was very influential in the "teaching" of values in the 1970s.

These educators focus on the process of valuing—the act of stating one's values—rather than the content of the values. The method is applied to moral values (such as euthanasia), as well as to other social values (what clothes, cars, and music one has). In values clarification, values are based on the processes of choosing freely (thoughtfully from alternatives), prizing (being satisfied with the choice and willing to affirm it publicly), and acting (doing something repeatedly with the choice). The concept of value results when these criteria (processes) are satisfied. In other words, a value results when I freely choose (to violate the dress code), prize (people will think I am cool for taking the stand), and act on a value (challenge the dress code daily).

The key technique involved in values clarification is the clarifying response. A clarifying response is a teacher's way of responding to what the students say or do in order to get them to reflect on what they have chosen, or what they prize ("Is this what you believe?"). The primary intent of the clarifying response is to get students to look more closely at their behavior and their ideas about behavior. Stating one's value is of paramount importance. Moralizing, critiquing, or evaluating a student's stated value by the teacher or other students is to be deliberately avoided. The following represents a possible exchange:

"Bobby, how do you feel about the mother grounding the child because he got low grades?" asked the teacher.

"I would hate her!" replied Bobby.

"Bobby, why do you feel this way?"

"It isn't right. The boy should be able to play. School is separate from home."

"Bobby, thank you for sharing your views! Who else wants to share?"

We all have heard these types of exchanges in classrooms that use values clarification strategies. What is important within values clarification is the act of stating one's values, not whether one's values have any merit or whether the values one expresses or practices could help a person develop a good character or be a good citizen or neighbor. The act of stating the value gives credence to the value. I think this notion is ridiculous. Bobby's pronouncement about how he would feel about his mother is wrong. We must recognize that his language to express his feelings may be limited, and he may be angry about something that happened in his home and is transferring this to the value situation. Still, he should be told that his statement is inappropriate. Hating is wrong.

One could point out to the child why this is wrong and ask the student to consider the implication of individuals who act in a hateful way toward others. One could share some readings with a child that illustrated how hating someone never solves a problem or heals the hurt of one who hates. Furthermore, a child's school activities are linked to his home activities. Inappropriate actions in school should have reasonable consequences in the home. A teacher who would allow the exchange noted above to pass without comment would probably state that all values are equal. "My values are as good as your values!" A belief in such nonsense would not allow a teacher to correct the moral "reasoning" of a child. Unfortunately, some educators believe their role does not include correcting intellectual inconsistency or helping to develop the character of children.

There is little question that values clarification methodologies have had considerable impact on teachers and curriculum development. They have been helpful in encouraging students to think about their own personal commitments and beliefs—the mental models they bring to the classroom and through which they interpret the world. The method also encourages students to listen to others and reflect on various alternatives. But there are at least five serious difficulties with the values clarification methodology.

First, there is a basic relativism underlying Raths' approach. The philosopher Charles Taylor noted, when discussing Allan Bloom's ideas contained in *The Closing of the American Mind* (1987):

[Bloom's] stance was severely critical of today's educated youth. The main feature it noted in their outlook on life was their acceptance of a rather facile relativism. Everybody has his or her own "values," and about these it is impossible to argue. But as Bloom noted, this was not just an epistemological position, a view about the limits of what reason can establish; it was also held as a moral position: one ought not to challenge another's values. That is their concern, their life choice, and it ought to be respected. The relativism was partly grounded in a principle of mutual respect. (pp. 13-14)

In other words, the relativism was itself an offshoot of a form of individualism, whose principle is something like this: Everyone has a right to develop their own form of life, grounded on their own sense of what is important or of value. People are called upon to be true to themselves and to seek their own self-fulfillment. What this consists of, in the last instance, each person must determine for him or herself. No one else can or should try to dictate its content (pp. 15-16).

Bloom's recognition that what far too many individuals recognize as a "right" is what the individual feels to be right, separate from an appeal to moral or intellectual tradition. Having a feeling about an issue, however, does not mean one has adequate information to make an informed decision. Take the example of the lifeboat dilemma. There are seats for 20 on the lifeboat but 21 who wish to enter. Students were asked, based upon a description of each of the potential passengers, to select who would be omitted from the boat.

I shared with my father this dilemma and he was astonished. "How could any child make such a decision? Why would anyone give this to children?" My father is an Iwo Jima-experienced Marine who knows the value of life, as well as the difficulty adults have when they must make such decisions concerning life and death. He recognizes, too, decisions a wartime doctor must make when there are too many wounded and not enough surgeons, but to ask this of a child with limited life experiences and philosophical and theological training is absurd. I agree with him, and yet this type of scenario was just what the values clarifiers would use—and is still used by some teachers today. Simply feeling that something is right does not make it right. Making good decisions in the best of times demands knowledge and experience. In the most demanding times, decision making may require the wisdom of Solomon. Teaching children that all decisions are equally valid is absurd. That would mean the Delaware teenagers who delivered their illegitimate baby in a motel room, killed it, and left it in a Dumpster in 1998 had a moral right to do so.

Second, many of the values clarification activities tend to emphasize conformity rather than personal, social, or moral development. John Stewart, in a critique of values clarification in the *Phi Delta Kappan* (1975), offers a sharp but accurate criticism of the values clarification approach, stating that there is a "coercion to the mean." Pressure is put on students to avoid taking the extremes of any position. Stewart notes that many of the extreme alternatives offered by values clarifiers are so value-specific and so emotionally loaded as to preclude them as legitimate alternatives for public affirmation by many people. For example, one item contrasts Virginal Virginia, who wears white gloves on every date, and Mattress Millie, who wears a mattress strapped to her back. The likelihood students would choose either of these two is remote. Their tendency is to avoid the peer pressure associated with the extremes and to take a middle position. (Another difficulty with this scenario is that individuals who choose to preserve their virginity are placed in an extreme position, although this may be the most ethical and healthy position to take.)

Third, choosing a value after thoughtful or reflective deliberation is emphasized, but what does it mean to "consider thoughtfully" a consequence? How does one do this? Are we engaging in sound moral reasoning with established moral criteria (such as religious or philosophical teachings) to assist us in making choices, or are we using reasoning in which self-interest is the norm? This is critical. We all have self-interests. Individuals may desire a raise in pay but recognize it would be unethical to sabotage someone else's work to receive the raise. There are criteria we should use to develop good moral decisions. With values clarification, one message being sent to students is that to consider a situation thoughtfully, one needs to have one's self-interest as the chief goal. As mentioned earlier, I have heard children say that it's okay to cheat as long as they're not caught. Another way of saying this is that self-interest trumps moral standards. This approach can also be seen in lobbying groups that seek to advance their self-interests without reflection on how their requests could affect others. How does this approach play in a society that requires some sense of self-sacrifice in order to further the needs of the group or society?

Fourth, the approach assumes that students are capable of discussing and deciding what is moral without a criterion by which to judge or assess their pronouncements. The assumption is made that all students have values, which they do, and that in a pluralistic society all values should be treated with respect, and all values are equal. Nonsense! Should Bobby's values toward a mother grounding a child merit any serious consideration? Many parents ground their children to help reinforce traits such as being respectful or responsible—and develop their character. They feel that there are times when punishments or consequences can result in a time for a child to reflect on what he did—which optimally will stop his inclination to continue this type of action in the future. Why should anyone respect or even acknowledge an espoused value that would go against the basic norms of decency and civility? Why should one accept a value statement that indicates a lack of concern for the welfare or betterment of society? But a teacher has no choice in a values clarification classroom since all values are equally important and have merit. Since values represent preferences, they are not necessarily tied to a moral standard.

Schools are not the only place where this occurs. Look at the glut of television talk shows. Popular television and radio talk-show hosts assume that if we talk about issues and listen to everyone's side and position, then we will come to understand and appreciate alternative views—thus, presumably, making us more moral since we'll understand another's point of view. Clarifying the value is more important than examining the value. Of course if all television talk shows reflected a decorum of civil decency, many of the hosts would be out of their jobs.

Fifth, there is no research evidence to substantiate that values clarification improves one's ability to think or reason in a morally consistent manner. Simply stating what I feel about an issue does not make me a moral or good person. It simply means that I have stated what I believe or feel. Consider the dangers of blindly accepting all values, with no value having greater merit than another. My values are just as good as yours, no matter what they are! The Ku Klux Klan's values of hate, intolerance, and violence are proudly passed on to the children of their members. Do we find that morally acceptable? The issue is not whether individuals have values. Everyone does. The issue is whether an individual's core values are consistent with principles of moral behavior and action, including both philosophical and religious influences. Remember, the values clarification approach emphasizes discussion and public affirmation—but not accuracy, consistency, or morally acceptable and reasoned responses.

In conclusion, values clarification does not do what it is supposed to do. It fails to present a moral ideal. Charles Taylor notes in *The Ethics of Authenticity* (1991): "What do I mean by a moral ideal? I mean a picture of what a better or higher mode of life would be, where 'better' and 'higher' are defined not in terms of what we happen to desire or need, but offer a standard of what we *ought* [my emphasis] to desire." (p. 16)

Kevin Ryan and Anne Bohlin, in their fine book *Building Character in Schools* (1999), recognize the educational pronouncement of the value clarifiers and distinguish between values and virtue. Their discussion has importance in our reflection on values clarification. Values are what we desire, what we want, and what we ascribe worth to. They can be reduced to a matter of taste or feeling rather than representing the product of thought and deliberate choice. Furthermore, values can be good *or* bad (p. 35).

They note that values can include personal tastes in clothing or cars, as well as values shaped through social, ethnic, and cultural customs, and religious, ethical, and philosophical traditions. Ryan and Bohlin contend that the question of values is not simply which values one holds, but the more important issue of the authority of value statements.

> The current cultural climate holds that values are not only a matter of choice, but also a personal right, not to be limited by some sort of "moral authority." Each person is free to define his or her own values. This works fine when we limit ourselves to questions of taste, as in "I really value evenings by the fire," or "I like dry white wine," but such subjectivism can become pernicious in the moral realm. Does anyone have a right to value, say, using manipulation and power to get their way with people? For the cultural relativist, rules are man-made and thus quite arbitrary. Adherents to this view allege that if everything is relative, there are no moral principles and no universal good to count on. In our ethnically, culturally, and religiously diverse society, we have moved swiftly from cultural relativism to personal relativism. In the world of personal relativism, the individual is king. Confronted with an ethical problem, we are responsible for solving it only in the way it suits us best. We are our own private judge and jury. (p. 36)

The authors continue arguing for the development of virtue in students. They recognize that values "evoke neither a moral commitment nor the promise of leading a good life." While "virtue is both the disposition to think, feel, and act in morally excellent ways and the exercise of this disposition…as a means, virtues are those habits and dispositions that enable us to live out our responsibilities more gracefully." (p. 45)

Are we splitting hairs here? I think not. What Ryan and Bohlin have pointed out is that virtue requires a standard by which conduct is assessed and a willingness to live and be judged by that standard. It goes far beyond what I value and focuses us on what, as Taylor notes, "ought" to matter. Building this "ought" requires a reflection on the cultural mores and the intellectual tradition of thousands of years. This can be done within a great deal of divergency.

> The devout Southern Baptist who is trying to follow Jesus and the agnostic struggling to make her life a work of art agree that they should be honest in their dealings, treat the underprivileged with compassion, and respect the rights of others. Further, as citizens of the same nation, they usually agree on certain moral standards and virtues that are instrumental in advancing the common good. (p. 41)

Values clarifiers and those who accept subjective relativism have no such standard. Their standard is personal and in that sense adequate. But a personal standard offers nothing in defining what we ought to do. There is a difference between examining values as personal and those as moral. The personal requires an appeal to taste. The moral requires an appeal to an intellectual tradition and recognized actions of rightness and excellence. It requires virtue or sound actions and thoughts. When the personal is treated as the moral, we have the miseducation of children. Values clarification represents the miseducation of our children. Today it's very hard to find an open advocate of values clarification, though its epistemological influence still affects some attitudes and teaching methodology. This is found especially in those educators who focus on self-esteem as an end in itself.

Values clarification—and its implied or accepted fixation on self-esteem—offers little to help communities grow and develop virtuous children and adults. So why should we even be discussing this approach that has so many obvious problems? Values clarification is still in many of our school systems, especially in counseling or self-esteem programs. Some teachers and counselors feel that they should not tell a student that one value is better than another. Such a teacher or counselor is supposedly avoiding "indoctrinating" the student. But all education is an attempt to indoctrinate! Our concern should be the virtues and skills with which we indoctrinate students, not whether we should indoctrinate. Programs that attempt to develop self-esteem in students are too simplistic and can be counterproductive in the formation of good character. (Kilpatrick, *Why Johnny Can't Tell Right From Wrong,* 1992) Such programs assume that if we can get students to feel good about themselves, then they will become good. Clearly this oversimplifies. Feeling good does not equate with being good—bank robbers feel good about having the money they stole! Having high self-esteem does not lead to acting in an ethical manner. I may feel good about myself for severely beating a member of another gang, but I doubt many of us would consider this any reason to feel good about who we are as a person.

Self-esteem development programs also send the message that self-esteem comes from how I feel about myself, not from achievements based on hard work. In reality, self-esteem cannot be given to a person. It must be earned, and it is earned through the development of self-control, which allows a person to set and accomplish goals. The teacher's role is to establish a climate where the student can learn and practice right from wrong; work for social, moral, and academic improvement; and achieve these through his or her efforts. This is how to develop self-esteem. Programs that seek to build self-esteem through quick fixes, or without the requirement of hard work and sacrifice, are far too simplistic and narrow-minded. They equate feeling good with being good. William Damon notes in *Greater Expectations: Overcoming the Culture of Indulgence in Our Homes and Schools* (1995):

> In and of itself, self-esteem offers nothing more than a mirage for those who work with children. Like all mirages, it is both appealing and perilously deceptive, luring us away from more rewarding developmental objectives. While capturing the imagination of parents and educators in recent years, the mission of bolstering children's self-esteem has obscured the more promising and productive possibilities of childrearing. We would do better to help children acquire the skills, values, and virtues on which a positive sense of self is properly built (p. 72)

Parents and teachers alike should be very wary of programs that promise to develop a child's self-esteem. The impact of values clarification is not limited to self-esteem programs. I have noticed that some social studies teachers profess that all cultures should be given equal respect, that all cultures have equal value and merit. Cultures and principles that are developed to guide individuals and nations are not all equal. We should study about other cultures and teach students to respect the beliefs of other cultures, but this does not mean we should value them all equally or recognize other principles of governance as equal to a democratic tradition. For instance, I have difficulty justifying a culture that would practice female circumcision. I acknowledge that it exists, but I cannot recommend it as a model for the development of the rights of women. I consider it horribly abusive. This does not mean that everything is always perfect within the Western intellectual tradition, or, for that matter, in democratic countries in general. Principles are guidelines for action, but they are not always followed. The maltreatment of blacks and native Americans and the internment of Japanese-Americans during World War II are examples of governmental decisions in which the principles of our Constitution were not followed. Nevertheless, history notes that some of these wrongs have been redressed to some degree. To redress, one must appeal to principles or ideas that force us to examine present conditions and ask whether there is a better way. We appeal to principles or moral standards to act as a guide.

There are moral standards that we can apply to assess and judge our actions. It may take time to learn and teach these standards, but they do exist. They are found within the religious and philosophical writings over the last 2,400 years. C.S. Lewis, in his book *The Abolition of Man* (1947), compared the ethical pronouncements of various religions and philosophies from all over the world. In his work he noted common considerations regarding honesty, kindness, loyalty to others, charity, and other standards that enhance the moral life. Our question as educators is not one of standards or preferences, but rather to examine which standards we have and if one standard is better than another (i.e., does one standard uplift humans compared to one that degrades humans?).

Dr. Martin Luther King, Jr. illustrated the application of moral principles in his "Letter From Birmingham City Jail," written while he was incarcerated for leading his civil rights activities. In it, he appealed to our Declaration of Independence, the Constitution, and ideologies and philosophical precepts within the Western intellectual tradition as the providers of the moral principles upon which his struggle for equal treatment for all Americans was based. In Tiananmen Square, the appeal of the Chinese students to the "Goddess of Liberty" was an acknowledgment of and yearning for these democratic principles; there were few, if any, appeals to the moral hierarchy of the communist Chinese government.

In conclusion, values clarification and its later evolution, the self-esteem movement, are not adequate to develop good character in our students. Both are self-centered, more concerned with individual wants than any sense of right action. Both are relativistic and devoid of intellectual and philosophical principles that would help establish a moral standard of good behavior and actions. Values clarification ultimately leads to a false sense of goodness with no grounding in reasoned standards that are uplifting to the human spirit. Ultimately it leads to a fixation on self-esteem, which is handed out in bushel baskets. This is a different animal than the self-esteem one earns through effort, sacrifice, and the losing of the self out of consideration for others.

It's ironic, but to develop real self-esteem, one must not focus on the self! It would seem, at least from a Platonic perspective, that we need an approach based on principles which state and affirm that some values are better than others and that there are widely accepted ethical and moral principles to guide this decision making. What might help is a philosophical approach to moral education. This is the approach taken by Lawrence Kohlberg.

The Cognitive Moral Developmental Approach

The work of psychologist/philosopher/educator Lawrence Kohlberg, *Essays on Moral Development: The Philosophy of Moral Development* (1981), represents a powerful response to the work of the values clarifiers. Kohlberg maintained there are principles that can guide our decision making in the moral domain. In this manner, Kohlberg is considered a "formalist." In his view, moral decisions could be made by appealing to principles, which are considered to be supreme. The highest level of moral reasoning would, therefore, appeal to principles, without consideration of the content of a particular situation. In other words, principles should guide our behavior, regardless of the content or situation surrounding the issue. If I adhere to the moral principle "Love your neighbor as yourself," it guides me in my behavior, no matter who my neighbor is (e.g., my neighbor may be a fool, but I will still respect him and honor his rights and privacy). Moral principles are therefore prescriptive—they prescribe what one ought to do and what would be considered a moral action.

Kohlberg accepted Immanuel Kant's formal principle: "Whether I could will that the maxim should become a universal law, governing not merely this particular action of mine, but the actions of all agents similarly circumstanced." In other words, the principle (maxim) that I take should become a guiding principle for other people. A maxim might state that I, and all other individuals, should treat people with respect, and that we should not use others to achieve our selfish interests.

Kohlberg also recognized the work of John Rawls, *A Theory of Justice* (1971). A crucial point within Rawls' argument is the concept of the "veil of ignorance." Roughly, Rawls argues that moral decision making about the obligations of a society should be undertaken without knowledge of the position one will play in a society. For example, if I were a lawmaker, I should ask myself if a proposed bill to raise taxes should be passed into law even if I were too poor to pay them. Would this be a fair law for all people? One would need to reflect on the advantages and disadvantages as an outside observer by asking, "If I didn't know the position I would have in society (i.e., fortunate or poor), would this still be a good law?" The decision one makes should represent what one would wish anyone to make facing the same situation. In this manner, the principles established are based on rational arguments, not the status, whether wealthy or poor, of the observer. Kohlberg's theory represents a strong philosophical tradition. However, he has added an interesting twist to his theory, combining philosophical traditions as prescriptive and cognitive developmental theory as descriptive—or how one learns to reason and act in a moral manner.

Kohlberg approached moral development by building on the work of the noted cognitive developmental psychologist Jean Piaget, who stated that there are stages, or steps, of cognitive moral development. The ability to think and reason about moral issues is dependent, to a degree, on the psychological maturity, or stage, of the individual. Stages are rather fluid, not rigid. As an example, we recognize that children go through various stages such as the "terrible two's" or the "trying three's." When we speak of children being in either of these stages, we have an idea of their intellectual and emotional capabilities and actions. This does not mean that a child who is three never exhibits behaviors we noticed at two. It just means that the child is exhibiting more behavior that we commonly associate with three-years-olds. The linguistic use of the term "stages" helps us communicate about behavior or intellectual abilities of children and adults at a particular age.

In *The Moral Judgment of the Child* (1965), Jean Piaget postulated two stages of moral reasoning. The first stage, called the heteronomous stage, reflects a morality of constraint and is based upon a sense of respect and fear. Since children are unable to understand the relationship of moral rules to society, they obey rules because they want to please adults or avoid their wrath. A five-year-old may avoid taking money from his mother's pocketbook because he does not want his mother to catch and punish him. He may not consider that it is morally wrong to take from others for selfish gain. His biggest concern is that he will be punished if caught.

From the heteronomous stage, children move to the autonomous stage. As children get older, they begin to understand that rules are established and followed due to a sense of awareness of the rights of individuals. At the autonomous stage the older child begins to develop an awareness of rules as providing a sense of justice and cooperation rather than strict obedience for the sake of obeying the rules (i.e., I obey the rules because these rules are good for society and for people in society, not because I am afraid that I will be punished if I don't). A child at this stage does not take money from his mother because he knows that stealing is wrong, and if everyone stole, a civilized society could not exist.

A difficulty in all stage theory is that children may not be completely in one stage at any particular time. They seem to slide from one stage to another, with one stage, the dominant stage, predominating their reasoning and actions. For example, a child may recognize that if kids stole money this would be morally wrong, and yet this child may say it's okay to take some candy once if one does not get caught.

Kohlberg felt that Piaget was correct in acknowledging stages of moral reasoning or development. Based on his research, however,

Kohlberg recognized and described six stages of moral reasoning, which reflect a movement from very simple ways of "moral" thinking to a more complete theory reflecting the philosophical precepts of the Western intellectual tradition. The stages are summarized below:

STAGE 1: PUNISHMENT AVOIDANCE. The child acts to avoid punishment. If I can avoid getting caught taking cookies from the cookie jar, then it is acceptable to take the cookies.

STAGE 2: RIGHT ACTION CONSISTS OF SATISFYING MY NEEDS AND OCCASIONALLY THE NEEDS OF OTHERS IN RELATION TO MY OWN NEEDS. I will play with you if you agree to help me fix my bicycle. I have to give in order to receive, and that motivates me. I will help my dad sweep out the garage because I know he will play ball with me later.

STAGE 3: GOOD BOY/GOOD GIRL. I act to please others. We are good to each other because we are friends and members of the same group. The needs of the group determine my decision to go to the football game. I follow the rules of the family because I like to be considered a good son.

STAGE 4: FOLLOW RULES TO MAINTAIN SOCIAL ORDER, NOT BECAUSE ONE FEARS PUNISHMENT. I obey the rules of society because if one does not obey rules, anarchy could result. Rules give society order. I also obey the rules of my family because the rules allow the family to remain strong.

STAGE 5: RIGHT ACTION IS BASED UPON THE NEEDS OF THE MANY. Rules in school and home are developed to provide the best learning/living environment for as many people as possible. I realize that laws should be changed if people are not being treated equally under the laws.

STAGE 6: SELF-CHOSEN ETHICAL PRINCIPLES. What is right must apply to everyone. Rational principles such as treating people as ends, not as means to ends, guide my thinking. Laws should be established so that all individuals are guaranteed equal rights and privileges based on what rationally should be desired.

Kohlberg determined individuals' stages of moral reasoning by asking them what they would do in an assigned dilemma. The most famous one is called "Heinz' Dilemma."

> In Europe, a woman was near death from a very bad disease, a special kind of cancer. There was one drug that the doctors thought might save her, a form of radium a druggist in the same town had recently discovered. The drug was expensive to make, but the druggist was charging ten times what the drug cost him to make. He paid $200 for the radium and charged $2000 for a small dose of the drug. The sick woman's husband, Heinz, went to everyone he knew to borrow the money, but he could get together only about half of what it cost. He told the druggist that his wife was dying and asked him to sell it cheaper or let him pay later. But the druggist said, "No, I discovered the drug and I'm going to make money from it." Heinz got desperate and broke into the man's store to steal the drug for his wife. (Kohlberg 1981, p. 12)

After reading the dilemma, people are asked to evaluate whether Heinz should have taken the drug; was it right or wrong? Yes or no answers to this question, however, do not provide insights into the level or potential stage of a person's moral reasoning. They only provide the preference. What is crucial are answers to the next question: "Why do you think that?" The reasons subjects give to support their choices within the so-called "Moral Judgment Interview" allow the trained interviewer to assess the subject's stage or level of moral reasoning. This is a complex task, which usually requires numerous follow-up questions and sensitive interpretations.

Kohlberg felt that one could predict how people would act in various situations based on their replies. Those who studied under Kohlberg and others who were influenced by him began to question if it were possible to facilitate the development of moral reasoning by a program intervention—to move people from lower to higher stages of moral reasoning. Researchers began to study the topic. For example, if a group of children were judged to be at Stage 2 ("I'll clean up around the school because the sooner I am through, the sooner I can have some fun."), a researcher would expose them to reasoning that a Stage 3 child might exhibit ("I am willing to help clean up around the school, because my friends and teachers feel it is a good idea."). In general, courses in ethics, and curricula or programs emphasizing a discussion of issues and exposing students to the next higher stage of reasoning resulted in an increase in students' moral reasoning.

In Vincent (1991), I assessed whether it was possible to facilitate moral reasoning through a semester-long course in ethics for high school students that had them use primary readings and commentaries from various philosophers. The students discussed these readings in seminars and small groups. Each student wrote one major paper involving an ethical issue and kept a diary of thoughts. The topics were introduced via a Philosophical Problem Sheet. Introduced in my book, *Philosophy for Young Thinkers* (1987), co-written with Joseph Hester, the following is one example, used to help students understand the difficulty of the separation of church and state:

Snake Eyes

A judge is presiding over the trial of the State vs. The Holiness Church. The Holiness Church handles snakes as a part of its worship service. The State is seeking to stop this practice. Meanwhile, the defense argues the prosecution is violating the separation of Church and State, which is guaranteed by the Bill of Rights under the Constitution.

The prosecution argues that the snake-handling church puts its own members and other citizens who attend the church in a dangerous position. Individuals who handle poisonous snakes during the worship service could be bitten and be unable to get to a hospital or perhaps choose not to go. The State further argues that taking children to this worship service, even if they were not bitten, could prove psychologically harmful to them. Outside the church, a child's peers could judge the child as bizarre for attending the church. Peer isolation could occur, which could make the child feel that he or she is not liked. Such children could suffer developmental trauma.

The church defense argues that their command to handle snakes comes from the Bible. They cite Mark 16:17-18 as their source: "And these signs shall follow them that believe: In my name shall they cast out devils; they shall speak with new tongues. They shall take up serpents and if they drink any deadly drink, it shall not hurt them; they shall lay hands on the sick and they shall recover."

The church considers the Bible to be the supreme lawgiver. It is the Word of God and should be obeyed. Should a snake bite someone, it is considered to be God's will. In answering the point that snake handling in church is psychologically harmful to children, the church's lawyer responds, "How could God's Word be psychologically harmful? God's Word conquers all and must be obeyed. In addition the children are not allowed to handle and are kept away from the snakes until they reach adulthood."

Finally the church defense appeals to the U.S. Bill of Rights under Amendment 1: "Congress shall make no law respecting an establishment of religion, or prohibiting the free exercise thereof...." It would appear to be a violation of Amendment 1 if the State were to attempt to outlaw the handling of snakes within a worship service. The state has no right to interfere with what goes on during a church service. At this point the defense rests its case. (pp. 112-113)

The students then participated in activities designed to recognize the philosophical issues in the lesson. This practice preceded the reading of primary sources and seminar discussions. The intent of the Philosophical Problem Sheet was to give students a cursory understanding of the issues before introducing them to more demanding primary sources. After studying primary and scholarly comments on various issues and doing activities designed to insure the students understood the primary and scholarly commentaries, the students participated in a seminar or group discussion, which attempted to enlarge the students' understanding through a sharing of ideas. This was not a generalized session. Students had to defend their ideas by appealing to the texts. They had to consider the needs of others and reflect on various philosophical positions. For some students it was the first time they had been asked to support their conclusions based on readings and not just opinions or feelings. The course was intellectually rigorous and yet the students did their readings and loved the seminars.

Using this approach, the students taking the course increased nearly one stage in their moral reasoning ability as measured by James Rest's Defining Issues Test, a multiple-choice test designed to measure stages of moral reasoning. It would appear that the use of dilemmas with carefully designed activities does have a role to play in educating for moral reasoning. Analyses of studies by Alan Lockwood (1978), James Leming (1981), and James Rest (1986) also suggest that it is possible to facilitate the moral reasoning of students as measured by Kohlberg's and Rest's assessment tools.

So what does it mean to facilitate the moral reasoning of individuals? For one thing, Kohlberg and other researchers have shown through many studies that those who are at higher stages of moral reasoning, as indicated by Kohlberg's Moral Judgment Interview or by Rest's Defining Issues Test, tend to respond to situations and various experimental programs in a manner that would be considered by the evaluating researchers as acting in an ethical manner. Following are several examples.

In the famous Milgram study (1963), participants were ordered to administer shocks of up to 450 volts to an "innocent victim" who was sitting out of sight in another room. Actually, no shocks were administered. Trained actors pretended to receive the shocks. The real subjects were those administering the shocks. Though the subjects administering the shocks in increasing doses could hear the "victim" scream, the experimenter would urge them on. Based on a series of experiments, Milgram determined that 65% of the subjects would follow the commands of the experimenter and continue shocking the "victim" no matter how loud the victim's protests. The protests could escalate to a pounding on the door and screaming in pain. Two-thirds of the participants were willing to administer strong enough shocks to actually kill the "victim"!

Kohlberg gave the Moral Judgment Interview to 26 undergraduates who participated in an early version of the Milgram study. In a later rescoring of the interviews, Kohlberg (1984) noted: "[N]early all subjects (87%) at the highest stage (in this study, Stage 4) quit. This compares to only 6% of those in transition from Stage 3 to 4." (p. 546) A possible explanation is that individuals who are between Stages 3 and 4 are still oriented toward wanting to please the authority figure (the experimenter), compared to those who have reached Stage 4 and can reason based on the needs and expectations of a good or just society.

In a follow-up investigation, S. McNamee (1978) offered a stooge who posed as the next "victim" in the experiment. The stooge stated that he had taken drugs and was having a bad experience. The experimenter said that she was a research psychologist, not a therapist, and that the experiment should proceed. The drug-user persisted in soliciting aid. The subjects then had to decide whether to help the drug-user or not. In the study, 75% of those rated at Stage 5 offered to help the stooge, while only 38% at Stage 4, 27% at Stage 3, and 9% at Stage 2 offered help. McNamee also observed that three-fourths of the subjects reasoning at Stage 3 stated, in a hypothetical situation, that a person in the stooge's situation should be helped, but only 27% of them actually offered help! Thus, individuals at Stage 3 may agree upon the social desirability of providing help, but most are unable to resist the command of the authority figure. McNamee's outcomes were similar to Kohlberg's results using Milgram's participants. Only at the principled level of moral reasoning is there a strong tendency for subjects to reject obedience and act by the principle of treating persons as ends having value and dignity in their own right. It may be that individuals at Stages 5 and 6 are able to react to novel situations because a moral response demands moral reasoning. The application of habit may not help individuals when they encounter novel situations, whether experimental or in real life. The ability to think and reason may be the key tool in guiding actions.

Kohlberg's approach is far more educationally and philosophically sound than the approach of the value clarifiers. He is able to show that there are stages of moral reasoning and that later stages are more adequate in helping individuals determine the principles and actions that most reasonable people would consider moral. The value clarifiers can make no such claim. In addition, Kohlberg builds on a philosophical tradition, starting with Socrates and Plato, which emphasizes a rational approach in the development of philosophical principles. Third, Kohlberg and various researchers building on his work have been able to show that the moral reasoning of individuals can be developed through certain kinds of educational programs. There is no evidence that values clarification facilitates moral reasoning of individuals. Finally, Kohlberg is able to show that individuals who are able to reason at higher stages, and therefore are concerned with the rights and needs of individuals, are able to apply these philosophical positions in experimental studies. Yet, there are other issues to consider.

When a colleague and I were discussing Kohlberg, he said that his mother would most likely rate a low stage of moral reasoning based on Kohlberg's scale. She would not be able to articulate or state reasons why one should do a particular action. His mother, however, is clearly involved with her community, working tirelessly to help others regardless of race, color, or creed. Her heart goes out to all people in need. When he asked her why she worked so hard all the time for others, she scolded him and told him that is what she was supposed to do. She emphasized that she had been doing this all her life, and that this is what people should do! He remarked that his mother was involved in helping others because she developed the habit of caring about others from her mother. She could not give a discourse in moral reasoning that would indicate a higher stage of moral reasoning. Yet no rational discourse was needed; she lived out an expression of moral reasoning in her habits. The same characteristic was recognized by Samuel Oliner and Pearl Oliner (1988) regarding those who chose to rescue the Jews during World War II.

Let us consider the issue of using "Heinz" and other dilemmas as the sole means of moral education. Dilemma, used intelligently by a skilled teacher, can play a role in focusing students on ethical issues. However, knowing what to do in a dilemma may not translate into knowing how we should treat people in day-to-day activities. In much of our lives, our moral lives, we do not need to resolve difficult moral dilemmas such as abortion or stealing drugs to help a sick wife or contemplating the separation of church and state. We are merely involved in trying to treat people in a civilized manner, caring about our neighbors and families, and trying to respond in a way that makes us a valued part of the community. The discussion of dilemmas, while interesting and potentially valuable in helping students recognize consistency in the development of thinking, probably has little to do with the everyday moral responses within our lives. Life is far too rich and complex to break down into a series of discussions or writings to determine the moral standing of an individual. Furthermore, a person can be exposed to the intellectual richness and moral arguments found in the Western intellectual tradition and still not be a good person. One can know what to do and choose not to do it. If the ability to reason about moral issues were the only prerequisite in developing the good person, then all philosophers would be our moral leaders. I'm not sure this is always the case!

One must examine the whole life, the actions as well as the words, of individuals. Edwin Delattre (1993) noted that a strict dilemma approach to moral education

> obscures the fact that relatively few of our normal moral failings and failures are attributable to inept reasoning about dilemmas. Many more arise from moral indifference, disregard for other people, weakness of

will, and bad or self-indulgent habits of life. We do, after all, sometimes know what we should do and fail to do it. If it were otherwise, then every philosopher who is good at moral reasoning would also be an admirable person. (p. 50)

Christina Hoff Sommers (1993) also recognized the problems involved in a strict dilemma approach to moral education. While teaching an ethics course at the college level, she exposed her students to various ethical positions such as Kantian formalism (Kohlberg's Stage 6) and utilitarianism (Kohlberg's Stage 5), a philosophical position that advocates providing the greatest good for the greatest number of people. Afterwards she had her students apply these theories to dilemmas such as abortion and euthanasia. She noted that her students developed the ability to argue the positions, but she questioned whether they were beginning to develop a good character—or to change their lives and act upon rather than argue about principles of morality and virtue. She changed her methodology and had the students begin to read Aristotle and discover the importance of developing a good personal character. Her students began to note that they could improve their own character through their readings and their actions. This was more appealing to her students than developing better arguments for the sake of arguments.

There is also the question of whether one who is able to reason at the higher stages of moral reasoning will be a good person. I believe that individuals who are capable of principled reasoning (Stages 5 & 6) will have insights into how to act in a novel situation different from the day-to-day experiences and expectations of life. In other words, the novel ethical issue demands higher levels of thought rather than just moral habits one has developed. Additional research is needed on whether this ability to think and reason at higher stages helps a person in his daily relationship with his family, neighbors, or members of the community. Since much of our moral life depends on the habits we have developed over the years, reasoning may not be enough to be a good person in deed and action.

Finally, we must consider whether teachers are capable of exhibiting the wisdom of Socrates in helping students understand the inherent difficulties of many ethical issues. This does not mean we should never consider difficult moral positions, especially at the high school level. A high school student should possess the ability to research, reason, and think about information at a higher level than elementary or middle school children. But discussion of these issues should be led by very capable teachers who are well grounded in philosophical thought, and we should acknowledge that these issues are best discussed by students who have already established the habit of virtue in their interactions with others. It is at this point that an experienced teacher can help students draw on their life experiences. However, this approach should not take the place of the study, analysis and discussion of literature, history, and philosophy as illustrators of those struggling to know and do what is right!

William Kilpatrick, in *Why Johnny Can't Tell Right from Wrong* (1992), offers an interesting proposition concerning the role schools should take in facilitating the moral character of children:

> Suppose your child's school was instituting a course or curriculum in moral education at the fifth- to seventh-grade level. As a parent which of the two models below would you prefer the school to use?
>
> *A.* The approach encourages students to develop their own values and value systems. This approach relies on presenting the students with pro-vocative ethical dilemmas and encouraging open discussion and exchange of opinion. The ground rule for discussion is that there are no right or wrong answers. Each student must decide for himself/herself what is right or wrong. Students are encouraged to be non-judgmental about values that differ from their own.
>
> *B.* The second approach involves a conscious effort to teach specific virtues and character traits such a courage, justice, self-control, honesty, responsibility, charity, obedience to lawful authority, etc. These concepts are introduced and explained and then illustrated by memorable examples from history, literature, and current events. The teacher expresses a strong belief in the importance of these virtues and encourages his/her students to practice them in their own lives. (p. 93)

Kilpatrick notes that the vast majority of parents choose proposition B; the majority of teachers choose A. Perhaps it is time that we have a meeting of minds on this issue. Many teachers have been indoctrinated by those professors who believe that values are personal, correct for that person, and hold equal weight with all other virtues. They learn in some schools of education to correlate feeling good with being good.

Proponents of other schools of education feel that schools should not attempt to "indoctrinate" children in virtues or character. Perhaps some teachers have been taught to stay out of the issue of character education.

Recently a colleague's husband had a counseling professor tell the class that there are no absolute rights or wrongs—only individual values that we must accept as right for that person. Those who advocate such an approach are wrong. Exchanging opinions does not create moral persons, although it helps develop a person's willingness to listen to the values of others. There is nothing essentially wrong with being courteous and listening to others, but there is something wrong with stating that everyone's values are equal and must be tolerated or advocated. Ethical relativism is not acceptable. Perhaps to work ourselves out of this quandary we should reexamine the work of Plato and Aristotle.

The Importance of Plato and Aristotle: The Foundation of a Solid Character Education Program

I believe that we can educate for good character, that we can develop students who are respectful, responsible, caring, and kind towards others in the school. We hope they can take this learning outside of the school and apply it toward others in the community. Throughout the country, schools are using various practices to help children develop good character. What we need is an assemblage of school strategies that can facilitate the development of moral character in our children. We need to reconsider some of the methods used in the past. We also need to apply what we know today that may help our efforts. But first we need to establish the foundation of such a program. Earlier, I briefly mentioned various religious traditions as guideposts to assist us in the development of character. Now I would like to turn to our philosophical tradition and briefly examine what the works of Plato and Aristotle say about the development of good character.

Thomas Lickona reminds us:

> The current debate in moral education—between those who stress thinking and those who stress experience or action—goes all the way back to Plato and Aristotle. Plato said that if a person really "knew" the good, he would be good. Aristotle disagreed, arguing that we become just by

the practice of just actions, virtuous by doing virtuous deeds. From Plato came moral education programs with an emphasis on improving thinking; from Aristotle, moral education with an emphasis on practicing right behavior.

To do an adequate job of moral education, one has to combine Aristotle and Plato. By itself, the Aristotelian emphasis runs the risk of producing outward conformity without inner conviction or understanding. By itself, the Platonic emphasis runs the risk of producing moral reasoning that does not carry over into moral action. (Quoted in Kurtines and Gewirtz 1991, p. 144)

To develop a child's character, we will need to develop the child's desire to do good by habit of action and by reasoning and thought. We must combine the insights of Plato and Aristotle.

According to Plato, one learned about being moral, as well as other aspects of the intellectual life such as clear, consistent reasoning, through dialogue or discussion. One could learn about moral character through a discussion of what constitutes good behavior toward others. For example, a student would advance a line of reasoning and argue for a particular position. We learned about this procedure through the dialogues of Socrates as written by Plato. The following excerpt from the dialogue "Crito" is typical of a Socratic dialogue. Socrates has been condemned to death for "actions against the state." Crito, a student of Socrates, urges his teacher to leave Athens and save his life. Socrates advances an argument that leaving Athens would be unjust. We pick up the dialogue as Crito and Socrates have just agreed that one should not return a wrong or an injury to another person, whatever the reason.

SOCRATES: Well, here is my next point, or rather question. Ought one to fulfill all one's agreements, provided that they are right, or break them?

CRITO: One ought to fulfill them.

SOCRATES: Then consider the logical consequence. If we leave this place [his prison cell] without first persuading the state to let us go, are we or are we not doing an injury, and doing it in a quarter where it is least justifiable? Are we or are we not abiding by our just agreements?

CRITO: I can't answer your question, Socrates. I am not clear in my mind.

SOCRATES: Look at it in this way. Suppose that while we were preparing to run away from here—or however one should describe it—the laws and constitution of Athens were to come and confront us and ask this question. Now that by this act which you are contemplating [escaping prison and leaving Athens thereby avoiding the death sentence] you intend, so far as you have the power, to destroy us, the laws, and the whole state as well? Do you imagine that a city can continue to exist and not be turned upside down, if the legal judgments which are pronounced in it have no force but are nullified and destroyed by private persons?

(Plato, translation 1961, p. 35)

Socrates continues by declaring that the state gave him life and helped provide a good life for himself and his family. Therefore to leave Athens would have been a violation of the law and would usurp the law, a law that he loves. Socrates chooses to stay and drink the hemlock rather than make a mockery of the state.

The successful promotion of Socrates' argument was based on its rationality and consistency. According to Plato, one learned about morality, as well as other intellectual pursuits such as politics and government, through the development of thinking and reasoning skills. Rationally, one could know what is right or wrong. Then, if one knows what is right or wrong, or knows the good, then one will do the good.

Aristotle, too, recognized the importance of knowing the good. He also noted the importance of practicing the good. In his *Nicomachean Ethics* we find:

Excellence or virtue, then, being of two kinds, intellectual and moral, intellectual excellence owes its birth and growth mainly to teaching, and so requires time and experience, while moral excellence is the result of habit or custom (*ethike*), and has accordingly received in our language [Greek] a name formed by a slight change from the word *ethos* (habit). From this it is plain that none of the moral excellencies or virtues is implanted in us by nature; for that which is by nature implanted within us cannot be altered by training....The virtues, then, come neither by nature nor contrary to nature, but nature gives us the capacity for acquiring them, and this is developed by training (Knoles and Snyder, 1968, pp. 45-46).

Aristotle recognized the importance of intellectual virtue, which is learned through teaching, reading, discussing, studying, and living.

He also recognized that it would take years to develop intellectual virtue, as indeed it takes time and experience to develop a sharp intellect. But what is as important to us is Aristotle's focus on moral virtue, or *the cultivation of habit as the tool to doing the good.* For Aristotle the development of good character was a learned skill, just as piano playing or boat building. One developed a good character by watching and emulating others who were caring, respectful, and responsible toward their family and peers. Note how this relates to the 18th-century character education efforts in the United States, which emphasized the use of community, elders, and apprenticeships. We hope that teachers and parents who are caring and respectful toward their students and children have students who mimic what they see. The copying of good behavior should facilitate the development of good character. This is an important consideration. Aristotle recognized that people live most of their lives in routine behavior. Most of us do not sit around contemplating whether everything we do has moral or ethical significance. We simply act, based on habits developed over a period of time.

In order to secure the opportunity to develop a good character, it is necessary to have a community or state that creates and supports morality through its legal system. For Aristotle, this is provided through social and legal structures. The state's ultimate purpose is to satisfy man's social instinct or instinct toward community. Individuals desire to live in groups, to socialize, and to live a good life, defined as a life lived out in the practice of virtues to others. Therefore, those who are involved in politics should exercise intellectual moral character (this is much closer to Plato's ideas since it emphasizes the application of the intellect) to provide for the citizen the best possible opportunity for living the good (moral) life. In this manner, just laws and social structures are established. The laws can be followed, taught, and practiced as habit. Aristotle states in the *Nicomachean Ethics*:

> It is difficult to get from youth up a right training for virtue if one has not been brought up under right laws; for to live temperately and hardily is not pleasant to most people, especially when they are young. For this reason their nurture and occupations should be fixed by law; for they will not be painful when they have become customary. But it is surely not enough that when they are young they should get the right nurture and attention; since they must, even when they are grown up, practice and be habituated to them, we shall need laws for this as well

and generally speaking to cover the whole of life; for most people obey necessity rather than argument, and punishments rather than the sense of what is noble. (1179b32–1180a4)

Although this may not be an uplifting appraisal of the human moral condition, it does make an important point. The role of government is to provide and develop just laws—laws that, when practiced until they are habitual, will allow the person to develop a good character, to practice civility and decency with and toward others. Laws that define the obligation of the state to the citizens should guide what citizens should provide for other citizens via the community. Just laws applied to the development of character should encourage the habitual development of just citizens, and sound educational practices in schools should contribute to the development of character of our students. The laws or rules and procedures as practiced become habitual and help develop civilities and courtesies in us all.

Conclusion

It seems we're back to Plato and Aristotle. With Plato, one develops the reasoning and thinking skills that are important in assessing and determining what is the moral good. Aristotle recognized that there were individuals who did not develop the skill of intellectual moral reasoning but lived moral lives through the development of habits they learned from others. Perhaps it is not a prerequisite that one *must* practice intellectual moral arguments to be good and kind, but one should be exposed to examples of morality. These can be working and association with others, as well as reading, analysis, and discussion of history, literature, and other means that illustrate individuals struggling to make good decisions on issues of ethics and behavior.

To develop moral students we must develop in youth the skills needed for effective thinking and reasoning, as well as the habits of good and right behavior that yield moral character. We must have both in our schools. Based on Plato's teachings, we should have schools that are dedicated to the development of the intellect as it relates to the ability to think, reason, and therefore respond to moral concerns.

Students, when they are intellectually able, should be challenged to think and analyze ideas and propositions within the school curriculum. Challenging topics may range from election rhetoric, to scientific cause-and-effect propositions regarding global warming, to issues concerning proper conduct, to an analysis of the moral precepts found in the Declaration of Independence and the Constitution of the United States. The nature of the discussions and assignment should reflect what we know about child development. Young children aren't capable of the same level of intellectual depth as older children, yet primary students are capable of discussing rights and wrongs, for example. They are capable of recognizing the kindness shown by Charlotte toward Wilbur in the children's book *Charlotte's Web*. Primary students will call upon their limited experience for discussion, while older students may speak just as much from ideas garnered from readings and discussions. Each age group, based on its intellectual development, is capable of analytical discussion.

The application of the moral virtue of Aristotle demands that we focus on developing good habits in children. Perhaps the philosopher R.S. Peters said it best: "The palace of reason has to be entered by the courtyard of habit." We should have schools where students see modeled and are able to practice virtuous habits such as respect, responsibility, and caring toward others within the school environment. Students should work with others of various ability levels and skills and practice helping and allowing themselves to be helped by others. Students should learn to assist others, not just academically but socially. For example, older students should model proper behavior for younger students to see and follow. Students should develop good habits in proper communication and courtesies, for they will be needed to show respect for others both in school and as they become adults. Students should have the opportunity to take responsibility for their work and their actions. In essence, schools should foster in students the habits and attitudes they will need to become productive, good citizens as adults.

How will the training of the intellect and the practice of good habits in students look in schools? There are five key components of a successful program, which are illustrated in the following graphic.

Note that teaching, modeling, and caring enclose the entire concept of character education, surrounding the five character components. And we must love our children. Period. This does not mean we will always like what they do. Educators must try to think of their students as their children. As parents, we may not always like what our children do. Sometimes we may be so exasperated we may temporarily

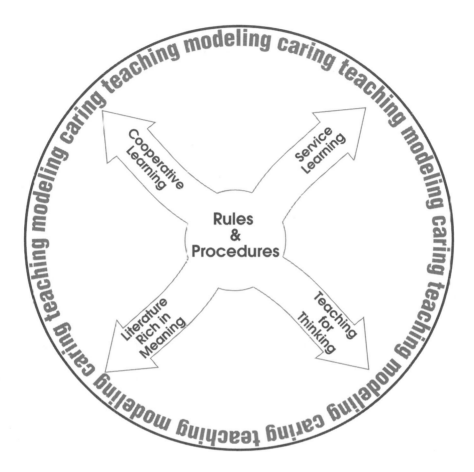

not like them, but we never stop loving them. The same is owed to our students. We must always try to love them. Every teacher must work hard to believe and practice this. Some teachers will have to practice loving students and hope there is a change in their own hearts! Still they must make the effort. Loving them means that we must model what having good character means. Actions speak so much louder than words.

We must always be respectful and caring toward our children. Being a caring person does not mean we let students get by with whatever they want to do. Caring demands far more than this. Caring for students demands that we become a compass—a moral compass to help them set the course of their lives—and that through our actions, exhortations, discussions, and daily examples, we help shape the character of our children. If we truly care about them, we must educate them not just intellectually but also in virtues such as respect, responsibility, and caring. With this always in the background, we can now briefly examine some specific practices that can be used within a classroom or school to help develop the character of students. Topics on the hub and spokes of the diagram on the previous page will be discussed in the following five chapters.

At the center of our diagram, and the most important element, are *rules and procedures.* We must establish consistent practices in school that show children the behavior that is expected of them. These practices help develop positive habits that will enable the student to be more successful both academically and socially in the school.

We must have students *learn cooperatively.* This places students in moral and social relationships with others and demands empathy and togetherness to complete projects or solve problems. It is important that teachers remember that students need to be taught how to work cooperatively.

If we are to help students learn to know the good, then we must *teach for thinking.* We want them to think clearly, to consider their assertions and have them assess them for consistency and ethical clarity. We must not stop at the practice of reasoning but must consider the ethical implications of our outcomes. Graphic organizers are helpful tools for teachers to use. They help students see and reflect on their thinking.

If it matters what students see on television and in the movies, then might it matter what they read. Students need to be exposed to *character-rich literature and narratives* that illustrate examples of "knowing, loving, and doing the good." Students and teachers must also go beyond simply giving rote answers to questions but must encourage deep discussions of readings worth discussing. Students must also be exposed to art and music as character development tools.

Finally children must engage in *service* both in the school and the community. I have found that children and adults benefit far more as servers than those being served.

Not one of these ideas calls for an add-on program. The simple reason for this is that add-on programs don't work. How many of you have time for a half-hour additional program in your day? You're probably lucky if there is time enough to teach the required curriculum. And take a look in your cabinets. Any discarded add-on programs in there? Besides we do teach kids attitudes and help them develop habits on a daily basis. Why not make it intentional? Why not make it positive and focused on teaching and modeling the virtues that are essential for living a good life?

To be successful, we must have character being taught within the "ethos" or life of the school. It is what we intentionally do, it is how we live. With the exception of service learning, all of the above are in place in schools today. Indeed for many schools, service learning is a part of the curriculum. What we must do is to utilize these strategies as tools to help students develop good character traits. In the next five chapters, I'll develop the concepts of these five strategies and how to adopt them as tools for character development. Chapter Eight will address implementation of character education.

My goal in writing this book is to excite your interest in developing a school that has character development as a focus. I have not gone into great depth in any area. To do that would require a much longer book. Indeed, entire books have been written on the topics briefly discussed in the following chapters. If you desire more information, and I hope you will, you will need to consult other sources, many of which are found in the bibliography.

Chapter 3

Achieving Civility in Schools:
The Merit of Rules and Procedures

Steve Dixon is the principal of Lilesville Elementary School in Lilesville, North Carolina, a rural, working-class town in the eastern part of the state. More than 60% of his students are entitled to free or reduced-price lunches. For some educators, having so many students come from very poor homes would represent an excuse for not succeeding in preparing them for higher education.

Fortunately for those families, this mind-set does not exist for Steve or anyone on his staff. They assume that all their students will be successful. This message is sent by the teachers, custodians, bus drivers, and cafeteria workers. Together they focus on modeling, developing, and reinforcing good habits in children. The result is a school where respectful, productive children behave responsibly, as they are expected to, and teachers readily complete the curriculum. The climate in Steve's school is one in which teachers dream of teaching, and in which students like to work hard. One look around Lilesville Elementary reveals that adults and students are respectful and kind to each other. When new students enter the school, other students model and teach them the procedures that help them fit into this climate. Lilesville is also a leader in the academic arena. In the most recent state assessments, the school far exceeded the score needed to earn "exemplary" status.

The educators at Lilesville Elementary attribute their success to their focus on character education, with an emphasis on rules and procedures. Doesn't this make sense? A school staff intent on modeling and developing responsibility, respect, kindness, and courtesy will be helping children develop traits essential to being successful and happy in life, not just at school. And as they bloom socially, they also bloom academically. Just ask Steve Dixon.

What Steve and his staff are doing is really what good parents do. If you value a clean house, you must teach your children to help you keep your house clean. If you value civility, you must teach and model civility for your children. If you value academic achievement, you must establish a time and place for study that become habits for your children. But children won't act in these productive ways unless they've been taught to do so.

What are the requisites for student success in schools? In my work in schools around the country, I've concluded that children's lack of success in school results in large part from their failure to develop habits needed to successfully complete work and become productive class members. This happens when a school—by which I mean principal, faculty, other school-based adults, and parents—fails to define and model the mission that academics and character development are *equally* important in a school. Failing to model traits such as being respectful toward others in words and actions—and not expecting students to learn and model these traits—punishes both teachers and students who desire and deserve school civility. Once students begin to develop the habits of punctuality, tidiness, respect, courtesy, responsibility, integrity, and perseverance, which are facilitated by the application of rules and procedures, they begin the process of becoming good students and good citizens, no matter what their socio-economic circumstances.

Good habits and character development are founded on obeying rules and procedures. Any longtime teacher will tell you that students' failure to develop respectful social habits and to follow rules and procedures can handicap them in developing their intellectual skills. And any company personnel director will tell you that failure of employees to follow rules and procedures will handicap their success in any career.

Not obeying rules can also stunt the social skills essential to being accepted by other children. What happens to students who fail to develop these good habits? Nancy Curry and Carl Johnson, in *Beyond Self-Esteem: Developing a Genuine Sense of Human Value* (1990), state:

> Being *good* or *nice* in middle childhood means two things. First, to be good in the classroom means to be well-behaved, hard working, and respectful of authority. *Bad* or *mean* children are disobedient, disruptive and lazy....[C]hildren who upset the teachers are often the same children

who are rejected by peers. Children who are hostile and lack self-control often fail to meet teacher standards of good behavior as well as peer standards of friendship. (p. 84)

The development of such skills will benefit the child in two important ways. First, she will develop skills needed for positive inter-action with other children. Through the development of good habits, the child will begin to internalize *why* she should act in a responsible manner. This process is facilitated if the teacher models and explains to the child why a particular behavior is required. For example, if a child is being disrespectful to another child, the teacher explains that this behavior is unacceptable. She then asks the child what an appropriate response might be, based on what respectful behavior has been dem-onstrated already in the classroom. Students respond better, as do adults, when they know why they are being asked to act in a particular manner.

The second benefit to the child is that developing good social habits will provide the thrust needed to succeed in school. Students who get along with the teacher and other students generally exhibit positive work and social habits. Jim Sweeney, in *Tips for Improving School Climate* (1988), recognized the importance of a positive school climate:

> Climate is a term used to describe how people feel about their school. It is a combination of beliefs, values, and attitudes shared by students, teachers, administrators, parents, bus drivers, office personnel, custodians, cafeteria workers, and others who play an important role in the life of the school. When a school has a "winning climate," people feel proud, connected, and committed. They support, help, and care for each other. When the climate is right, there is a certain joy in coming to school, either to teach or to learn. (p. 1)

The first and most important step in becoming a school that emphasizes respect, responsibility, and caring is establishing a positive school climate. A good climate reflects high expectations of behavior and provides support for children to develop these behaviors. James Kauffman and Harold Burbach (1997) recognize the importance of emphasizing basic civilities:

> At a minimum, the kind of social climate we envision is one in which everyone, teachers and students alike, treats others with consideration and respect and in which mannerly behavior and small courtesies are the

norm. More optimistically, we believe that a classroom where civility holds sway is one that is well on its way to facilitating classroom cooperation, responsible self-governance, and democratic living. (p. 322)

As the school climate of caring and civility grows, a safe and orderly environment should evolve, and academic achievement will rise. If a school lacks a positive climate, both intellectual and character development will face difficulty. This shouldn't surprise us. As adults, we like schedules and structure, especially within our work environment. It helps us do our work better when we know basically what to expect through the day and generally how those around us will act. Why should we desire anything less for our children? To establish a safe and orderly environment, we must first determine the characteristics that will guide us in the formation of the environment. Dr. Bill Rauhauser, an internationally recognized consultant in the area of effective schools, wrote in *The Planning Book of Effective Schools* (1993) the description of a safe and orderly environment:

1. The school climate reflects an atmosphere of respect, trust, high morale, cohesiveness, and caring.
2. There is a student handbook that clearly states expectations for student behavior.
3. A variety of classroom management skills are used to create a businesslike, orderly, and comfortable classroom environment, conducive to learning.
4. Discipline within the school is enforced in a fair and consistent manner.
5. Students come to class prepared. (pp. 9-10)

Rauhauser goes on to say:

There is an orderly, purposeful atmosphere which is free from the threat of physical harm. However, the atmosphere is not oppressive and is conducive to teaching and learning. It evolves from a commonly agreed upon school purpose and is characterized as positive and businesslike. (p. 60)

All educators want that orderly atmosphere because it lets them do what they got into teaching to do—to teach young people how to think and learn. Students want it too. The tough question is how to get your school there. The answer is rules and procedures. Until you tell children how you expect them to act, they will act the way they wish.

First, and most important for success, teachers and students must work together to develop rules and procedures for the classroom and the school. These will result in the development of good habits that promote good character. Essentially, if we want children to behave respectfully and responsibly, we have to explain to them what we mean by that. How will children know how we want them to behave if we don't tell them? It doesn't work that way in any home.

Let's define these terms in a workable context. *Webster's New World Dictionary of the American Language* (1986) offers these definitions:

> **Rule**: *an authoritative regulation for action, conduct, method, procedure, arrangement, etc.*

> **Procedure**: *the act, method, or manner of proceeding in some process or course of action; esp. the sequence of steps to be followed 2. a particular course of action or way of doing something.*

A rule is general, an objective—an example might be "Act with respect toward others." A procedure tells what to do to meet the objective of the rule—an example might be "Listen while others are talking."

Rules

What rules should a school have? How does a team working on developing rules and procedures set criteria for them? Here's a simple parameter: If a rule or procedure can help a student develop good habits of character, the rule or procedure has value. Harry and Rosemary Wong, in *The First Days of School* (1991), offer several suggestions on the establishment of classroom rules:

- The most successful classes are those where the teacher has a clear idea of what is expected from the students and the students know what the teacher expects from them.
- Expectations can be stated as rules.
- Rules are expectations of appropriate student behavior.
- After thorough deliberation, decide on your rules and write them down or post them before the first day of school.
- Communicate clearly to your students what you expect as appropriate behavior.
- It is easier to maintain good behavior than to change inappropriate behavior that has become established. (p. 143)

There are several ways to develop rules used in a school. Individual teachers may have rules specific to their classrooms, but it doesn't mean that each teacher is an island. Classroom rules should be congruent with school rules and generally consistent with other teachers' classroom rules. This helps insure a consistent, structured learning environment. The school rules reflect the overall climate aim of the school. They can be formulated by the entire faculty or through a study team of teachers, who report back to the faculty.

Rules should be established by teachers and students working together. Even primary students who have been in a good, nurturing environment know what is needed to help create a good classroom environment. They understand the importance of rules to establish standards of appropriate behavior. When we ask for their help and insight, we more readily get their cooperation. Does this mean that the student ideas for standards will always be accepted? No. It is the teachers' and administrators' job to insure a good learning environment and establish standards for behavior. We are the educational leaders, but leaders can learn from followers!

Chris Stevenson, in *Teaching Ten- to Fourteen-Year-Olds* (1992), states, that as educators we should guarantee to students that the rules "will be equitably derived, clearly articulated, and fairly enforced." (p. 211)

There should be two kinds of rules within a school. One type of rule, which the Wongs call a "specific rule," is descriptive in nature. Specific rules tell us what to do, such as: "Walk in the hall without talking in order not to disturb others." Some other examples of specific rules include:

1. Be in class on time.
2. Do not curse or use profanity.
3. Have all materials ready when class begins.
4. Hold the door for those walking behind you. (p. 145)

The other type of rule is called the "general rule," which offers overall guiding principles. "Do unto others as you would have them do unto you" is a guiding principle. We can grasp the objective—treat others the same way you would like to be treated—but the rule doesn't offer specifics on how to do that. General rules are very important in establishing a school's philosophy. They set standards that everyone can accept as appropriate for developing and maintaining a caring environment. Some general rules listed by the Wongs (1991) include:

1. Respect others.
2. Be polite and helpful.
3. Care for other members of the school family. (p. 145)

General rules are much trickier than specific rules because they are open to wider interpretation and may be difficult to reach a consensus on and to enforce. Perhaps in your school you have posted a version of this general rule: "Treat others with respect." Would students, staff, and teachers all have the same understanding of the practices that show respect for others? How much does that encompass? In order to make general rules strong and prescriptive to students (and to us), we must support the rules by adding expected procedures or practices that give more descriptive meaning to the general rules. Then the school rules can be consistently interpreted and consistently followed by everyone.

Procedures

Procedures are essential to the development of good practices or habits. To achieve the good practices, the procedures must be introduced and explained to the children, then reinforced through repetition and reminder. It works the same way in school as it does at home. Why would a child put his dirty clothes in the hamper unless he's asked to do so, sees other family members doing so, and is reminded to do so until it becomes ingrained habit? Similarly, a student won't walk quietly in the hall unless he's asked to do so, sees other students and teachers doing so, and is reminded to do so until it becomes ingrained habit.

Procedures give structure to all our endeavors, and most of our daily interactions. Coaches in all sports have players practice procedures (plays) so they'll be able to perform them when called upon, thus increasing a team's chances of victory. For instance, one doesn't learn how to turn a double play in baseball by being told how to do it, or by watching a video. One must *practice* it, and coaches drill their infields on this one play until the players can execute it—pow, pow! two outs!—almost without thinking. The soccer coach runs passing drills seemingly for hours, until the players' feet know exactly what to do. The brain is no longer needed for this small action because a good practice has been established.

The late, great educator Madeline Hunter suggested a wonderful procedure to use when students need help in a class. Each student is given a card with one side red and the other side green. As the students work, the teacher walks around the classroom. A student's card with the green circle up tells the teacher, "I'm doing fine and understand the work." The red circle turned up means, "I need some help. Please stop here." This is a good procedure that gets students help promptly with minimum disruption.

To use this procedure, a teacher could begin, "OK, students, look at me. I want you to practice using the red and green circles. Let us pretend you're working a math problem and you need some help. What color should you turn over on the right corner of your desk? Place the card on the right corner of your desk." The teacher would then go around the class to confirm that all students did it as asked. This may sound simple or elementary, but practice is essential if students are going to use a procedure regularly. (Note the value of the red/green circle procedure—the student doesn't need to raise a hand. Most students raise their writing hand, thereby stopping all work!) In addition, if all teachers in a school adopt the same procedure for seat work, it is transferred from one grade to another, thus becoming a school procedure.

The coaching and Hunter's examples are procedures that tend to promote good practices. Civility also arises from procedures. A high school math teacher spends time in each of his classes discussing with students the importance of civility in his classroom (and presumably the one they go to next). He has certain practices he expects of his students, which contribute to a good classroom climate:

1. Speak when spoken to. (He believes in greeting students individually when they enter the class and expects each student to speak to him.)
2. Raise hands and be recognized before speaking. In seminar groups, please signal to the moderator before speaking.
3. Practice small courtesies: Say "please," "thank you," "excuse me," and "I'm sorry" when appropriate.
4. Clean the area around your desk before you leave because it was clean when you sat down.

During the first week of school, and throughout the year as needed, he does various role-playing activities to reinforce these practices. He does it with a light touch and a good deal of humor, but the message is clear: "We will live according to these procedures, which will promote classroom civility. I will model them and I expect you to also."

Another example of establishing a procedure to indicate expected behavior would be explaining how to disagree with a point made in a seminar discussion without being disagreeable. The teacher might start by saying, "Attention please, students. Now we're going to learn how to disagree with someone's point of view in a seminar discussion. In the past I've noticed that some individuals seem to attack the person rather than what the person has stated. We have the right to disagree with someone's point of view. However, this does not mean we can say the person is stupid or doesn't make sense, or otherwise attack him. I'm going to role-play with you to demonstrate how disagreement should occur. Candace, I want you to give your opinion on whether Socrates should have accepted Crito's offer to help him flee the city in order to avoid prosecution."

Candace responds, "I think Socrates did the right thing by deciding to drink the hemlock. In the Crito, Socrates states he was living and therefore choosing to die by his principles."

The teacher raises her hand and acts as if she is recognized. "I disagree with Candace on this point. I think there's another issue here. If Socrates had truly loved the State, he would have escaped. The State would have avoided the embarrassment of executing him. My support is found in...."

The teacher is modeling with Candace the procedure that students should follow when they wish to disagree with someone's ideas or statements. Notice the procedure encourages students to show respect for others even though they disagree with their ideas. Won't it always be useful for them to know how to disagree without becoming disagreeable!

The same recognition of the importance of procedures can occur with young children in a school-wide focus. Several years ago I visited a Montessori school, which emphasizes the importance of grace and courtesy starting with children 2½ years old. For example, the children learn the procedure for opening and shutting a door. The children are taught how to enter a room, how to avoid having the door slam behind them. The children are also taught to shake hands—they practice a brief and firm handshake—with the directress and exchange greetings while looking her in the eye. They also address her when they leave.

Children also learn the procedures for interrupting another and practice the courtesy of saying "please" and "thank you." These procedures of behavior toward others are reinforced on a daily basis. In this way the Montessori school teaches, and in some cases reinforces what parents are teaching, regarding respect and responsibility in children's actions toward others.

The following are useful procedures that could be established during the first week of school:

HOW TO PASS UP PAPERS—This sounds simple, but much valuable time can be wasted when there is no orderly procedure for this common chore.

HOW TO PARTICIPATE IN CLASS DISCUSSIONS—Students need to know the procedures for participating in a class discussion. Do students need to raise their hands to speak? Can they interject their opinions when a lull occurs in the discussion without raising their hands? This needs to be clarified.

HOW TO GREET A VISITOR TO THE CLASS—Does the class have an individual from within the class who excuses himself from the class to assist a visitor? If so, is this person on a weekly or daily assignment to be the greeter? What kind of training does the class receive to accomplish this task?

Procedures should not be confused with discipline, which is an entirely different activity. The Wongs address the crucial issue of procedures, or practices, needed to implement the rules of a classroom or a school. They argue that the main problem facing the classroom "is not discipline; it is the lack of procedures and routines." (p. 171) They make a clear distinction between discipline and procedures.

DISCIPLINE—Has penalties and rewards.
PROCEDURES—Have no penalties or rewards.

DISCIPLINE—Concerns how students behave.
PROCEDURES—Concern how things are done.

In summary, rules and procedures are essential to the development of expectations and standards for students. The establishment of rules and procedures creates a positive classroom environment in which all students have the opportunity to succeed.

Developing Rules and Procedures

How does a teacher or planning team decide what rules and procedures to establish? How much of school life should be prescribed? What if not everyone agrees? Where do you begin making school-wide changes?

It will help to first develop a mission statement that confirms that character education is as important as the intellectual pursuits of the school. It can take time to reach consensus on this. Then, before starting to write rules and procedures, consider what the climate of the school should be like. Have teachers, students, and staff write down their descriptions. Many schools never achieve a climate of civility because their teachers and staff can't describe and model the behaviors needed to insure a civil environment for social and academic learning to occur.

Remember that procedures are more important than rules. For example, we can all agree on the importance of educators modeling and having students model and practice being respectful, responsible, and caring. What is needed is to define the practices that will make this a reality. It is critical for success for you to have consistency in your rules and procedures. Some individual teachers may already have their own classroom procedures. If a school rule is "No candy or gum," the rule will not work if one teacher allows gum in class.

I wrote how this process can be successfully completed by a faculty in *Rules & Procedures for Character Education: A First Step Toward School Civility* (1998). Briefly, teachers should work first individually, later within groups either by grade or subject, and finally as an entire faculty or representatives of the faculty to develop consistent rules and procedures. This helps insure consistency from the individual to the entire faculty. For example, the school staff may determine the general rule, "We will be respectful to others throughout the school environment." The staff will then need to determine the practices or procedures that will make this rule a reality. Select no more than five general rules, then develop the procedures to support them. Some procedures for an elementary school might be:

CLASSROOM
1. Raise your hand and be recognized before speaking.
2. Use polite language such as "please," "thank you," and "excuse me" when appropriate.
3. Listen attentively while others are speaking.

HALLWAYS
1. Do not talk in halls unless an adult talks to you.
2. Keep hands and feet to yourselves.
3. Hold the door for those walking behind you.

These procedures will need to be practiced throughout all classes and throughout the school environment. Involve your cafeteria staff in determining procedures for being respectful in the cafeteria and your custodial staff in setting procedures for school cleanliness. The same applies to the athletic department. By having the entire school focus on the practice of "respect," the message is sent that this is important to everyone and for everyone. Bill Rauhauser is fond of reminding his schools that "what is valued gets done." If modeling and teaching respect is valued, it will be done.

Children who feel successful in school, who know how to follow rules and procedures and know why they should, are more apt to engage in prosocial behaviors. By learning to follow, and perhaps even helping a school develop rules and procedures, students take the first step in helping insure a civil, caring environment governed by good habits that promote character development. Students should be encouraged to provide feedback about the proposed rules and procedures. Ownership can lead to acceptance.

Once consensus has been reached on the general rules and supporting procedures, a statement from the principal concerning the importance of rules and procedures is published and shared throughout the school. A copy of it also goes home to parents. Here's an example:

> We, the teachers, pupils, and administrators, feel that the development of a safe and orderly environment where students will learn and begin to develop the strategies needed to be successful in life, is essential for all students. With this in mind, we propose the following rules and procedures for all students in our school....

Consequences

Before concluding this chapter, we must note that not all students will do what is asked of them, even if a caring, discipline-centered environment has been developed. To insure a climate of civility for all those who follow the rules, there must be consequences for those who choose not to. Occasionally it's necessary to punish students, but it must be in a manner that is fair and non-abusive. With this in mind, physical punishment, such as paddling, should be avoided. I believe there are other methods, which are more humane and less controversial, that will accomplish the same goals. We must also seek to understand why a student is engaging in the antisocial behavior. Perhaps by understanding why the student is acting in a particular manner, we may be able to help the child engage in more appropriate behavior.

To be successful in this endeavor, we must establish a disciplinary policy. This must outline the consequences that will occur if someone continues to disrupt the civility of the school. James Q. Wilson in his book *The Moral Sense* (1993) reminds us:

> Testing limits is a way of asserting selfhood. Maintaining limits is a way of asserting community. If the limits are asserted weakly, uncertainly, or apologetically, their effects must surely be weaker than if they are asserted boldly, confidently, and persuasively. (p. 9)

This is confirmed in a large study recently released by the Educational Testing Service titled *Order in the Classroom: Violence, Discipline, and Student Achievement* by Paul E. Barton, Richard J. Coley and Harold Wenglinsky (1998). Utilizing baseline data from the National Educational Longitudinal Study of 1988, researcher continued to survey the students as 10th graders in 1990 and as 12th graders in 1992. Out of the original representative sample of 25,000, the researchers concluded the study with 13,626 students. The reduction was due to students dropping out, changing schools, or failing to participate in all three studies. Several of the study's findings are important for character education. Of particular interest is the relationship between maintaining order and the use of a sound disciplinary policy, which includes consequences:

> Another empirical assumption supported by this research is that the stakes in maintaining order are high. The consequence of student disorder is not merely more disorder; disorder also erodes the learning environment for all students as indicated by lower student achievement gains. Just as policymakers supposed, school order is closely tied to achievement. This finding suggests that disciplinary policy is not a side issue, distracting educators from more academic goals; rather, a sound disciplinary policy is a prerequisite for a sound academic policy. (p. 18)

Let me say it again, it's that important: A civil, orderly climate in a school enhances learning. I believe it's best accomplished by the establishment of good rules and procedures, which promote civility and order within the school. In my experience as a teacher, I've learned that the greater the civility, the better the academics. I also know that good practices sometimes are not enough to maintain civility. Therefore, I must establish and enforce consequences.

The finest and most logical discussion of punishment I have read is provided by Edward Wynne and Kevin Ryan in their book *Reclaiming Our Schools* (1993). The authors argue that for punishment or consequences to be effective, they must have certain characteristics:

1. They must be clearly disliked by students—they must deter.
2. They must not absorb large amounts of school time or resources.
3. They must be capable of being applied in "doses" of increasing severity.
4. They must not be perceived as cruel.
5. In public schools, they often must be applicable without strong cooperation from the parent of the pupil involved.
6. They must be able to be applied quickly—the same day, or even within one minute of the infraction, instead of next week. (p.88)

The authors recommend several consequences for poor behavior. Among them are phoning parents at work; subjecting pupils to before- or after-school detention within 24 hours of the offense; an in-school detention room where no talking is allowed among students and they are required to complete assigned work; sharply criticizing students (perhaps publicly); calling the police for criminal behavior; having students stand with their backs to the class and after a period of time making a public apology to the class; and suspension if needed. The authors suggest that to determine what consequences or punishments work, simply ask the pupils who have been on the receiving end if they would like to experience them again!

We can also develop a hierarchy of punishments. Several years ago I learned an interesting approach to increasing the doses of punishment from a middle school. The first level of discipline was having teachers walk around the classroom and make eye contact with students. They believed that one teacher on the feet was better than five in the seat. That eye contact became a stare for any child misbehaving or getting ready to (one funny teacher called this "giving them the evil eye"). If misbehavior persisted, a brief conference after class or after school was held with the student. If inappropriate behavior continued, the parents were called and their support requested. Most misbehavior stopped at this level, but the occasional student persisted. The next level of punishment was called "face the team," in which the student would have a discussion with his or her teachers, administrators if available, and a parent if possible. The student would sit alone, with the adults in a semicircle around him or her. The meeting was structured and clinical, with the goal of addressing why the child was choosing to misbehave. Such meetings were not easy for anyone, but at their conclusion, the adults would put their arms around the child and welcome him or her back into the school family. Very few students ever needed to go to the final step—suspension. This hierarchy of discipline was communicated clearly to the student body, and the administrators evaluate it as being very effective. The current average of office referrals in this 600-student middle school is one per day. It is also recognized by the state of North Carolina as a school of academic distinction.

Another approach to discipline involves the concept of restitution. In *Restitution: Restructuring School Discipline* (1992), Diane Chelsom Gossen argues that teachers should encourage children to seek solutions to problems that would normally demand teacher intervention or consequences. If a child vandalizes something, restitution would call for cleaning or repairing it, or if not possible for the child, working with the custodian on other cleaning activities. Say a child rips up another child's homework or calls someone a derogatory racial name. Instead of having the teacher punish the offender, the teacher has the offender consider what he can do to "make things right" with the child he offended. The offended and teacher must agree the restitution is appropriate. Restitution is not for all students and not for all situations. It's a option for students capable of acknowledging their wrongs and willing to make amends to the offended. It merits serious consideration for all schools wishing to help students assume responsibility for their actions. Since not all students are able or willing to admit a wrong, teacher-enforced consequences are still necessary, and some actions need quick consequences.

Students must know and understand the consequences that might befall them if they choose not to follow the rules and procedures. A list of possible consequences could be made available to students at the beginning of each year, so students know the outcomes for inappropriate behaviors. The guidelines should be flexible enough to allow some administrative decision making but specific enough so that students are aware of possible consequences for various unacceptable behaviors. Although consequences for poor behavior will always be needed, we can hope that the need for such measures will decrease as character-developing strategies are implemented.

Rules and procedures are at the center of all character-building efforts. They help the educators, students, and parents know the expectations of appropriate behavior and insure a climate of civility. Rules establish standards of excellence, and procedures establish the habits all students should strive to master. Developing habits that help children practice being respectful, responsible, and caring is crucial in the development of good citizens. Simply put, rules and procedures help educators and students practice being good.

Chapter 4

Cooperative Learning

Siecor, a wholly owned subsidiary of the Siemens and Corning Corporations, is the largest optical fiber cable-manufacturing company in the world. Its optical fiber cable is part of the rapidly changing "highway" on which communication—some of which we can't even imagine now—will flow. In the late 1980s, this highly successful company created an experimental work cell in its manufacturing process. Machines and personnel were moved out of each department to create a work team. The work team became a mini-factory because the entire manufacturing process of the cable could be completed within the team. Each member of the team learned to operate all the machines and had a complete understanding of the entire manufacturing process. Having the skills was not enough to insure a quality process. The teams worked cooperatively.

Since the entire manufacturing process was handled within one team, team members had to work together to solve problems. That required team members to respect their teammates and the "know-how" each brought to the team. Team workers also learned to take individual and team responsibility for the product outcome. Instead of blaming any one person for a mishap, all worked together to remedy it. The teams cared about the product and the individuals who made it. By working together creatively and developing ownership of the completed product, the workers illustrated the effectiveness of cooperative learning and working. The experiment was so successful that Siecor now applies the cooperative team process throughout plant operations in all of its manufacturing plants.

Siecor is a particularly innovative company, but more and more companies are moving towards a cooperative process of manufacturing and management. Specialists are becoming generalists. Interpersonal skills are now as important as technical skills and are sought in the interview process at many companies. There will be more of this kind of thinking in the new millennium. A person's ability to get along with others and to work cooperatively is becoming more important than what degree he has. To move successfully in this direction, business and manufacturing require individuals who are responsible for their work, respectful of the abilities of others, and caring about others and the product they produce.

In 1998, the New York Yankees amply demonstrated how it took every member of the team working together to insure success. No one individual carried the ball team—everyone contributed to make the 1998 Yankees become recognized as one of the greatest teams in baseball history. Success such as this, or regional success enjoyed by any athletic team, cannot occur without having a group of individuals learn to work smoothly together.

The University of North Carolina's basketball team was a consistent powerhouse for 30 years because Coach Dean Smith insisted on team play. Each newcomer had to learn how to fit into the existing unit, and if a player started to take over a game by trying to do it all himself, Smith pulled him out of play. As great a player as Michael Jordan was, he still played as part of a team at North Carolina—Coach Dean Smith wouldn't let him be a runaway star because it was more valuable in the long run for the team to work together. All those players understood that their organization was successful because everyone contributed to the effort. In a group success, no one is unimportant. All contribute. All are needed.

Families, schools, businesses, service organizations, sports teams, and the military all require people to work together to be successful. Homes are where this socialization and practice of cooperative learning and living begin. As children move from the home to the school, this role becomes a shared one. Cooperative learning in schools represents a valuable strategy in furthering the socialization of children.

The Role of Schools in Cooperative Learning

What exactly is cooperative learning? Gordon Vessels, in *Character and Community Development: A School Planning and Teacher Training Handbook* (1998), defines it as

> a group of techniques that gives students the opportunity to work together in pursuit of a common goal and to enhance their social, ethical, and cognitive growth in ways not provided by competitive-individualistic structures and traditional recitation-presentation methods. Cooperative learning methods differ in terms of their emphasis on true collaboration and the sharing of resources and whether they endorse competition and extrinsic rewards, but they commonly provide an alternative to traditional teacher-centered approaches to teaching. (p. 132)

Cooperative learning is learning both socially and intellectually in groups of two or more. It teaches children how to listen to others and help them solve problems, and to engage in activities that demand group rather than individual efforts to achieve success. It teaches them how to interact with those who think and express themselves differently. It lets them see how individuals differ in what they are good at. It prepares them to work and achieve results with a variety of people. Ask an experienced personnel director what one quality is the best indicator of an employee's success, and the answer you'll get is the ability to get along with others. Cooperative learning prepares children for life.

Spencer Kagan, author of *Cooperative Learning* (1992), reflects on the role that schools must play in the socialization of youth:

> Forces have combined to thrust on the schools—like it or not—the job of socializing our nation's youth. Schools must pick up the job of socializing students in the values of caring, sharing, and helping. Schools cannot stay out of the area of moral and social development. The evidence on this point is extremely clear. If exclusively traditional classroom structures are used, children become more competitive; if cooperative classroom structures are used children become more cooperative. And we must choose some type of classroom structure! The only real question is not if, but how, we are going to impact on the social development of our students. (p. 23)

This will not be an easy task for many schools. Some teachers still go into the classroom, shut the door, and begin to share their knowledge with the students. Students are judged and ranked by their ability to repeat the information. The focus is on retention of information and the ability to take tests, not application of the information. Although more apparent in high schools, this same practice is noticeable in elementary and middle schools as well. Often a school emphasizes competition and individual testing rather than cooperation among students. We need both—competition in athletics and academics and working cooperatively to meet group goals. But unfortunately, as long as educators feel that individual achievement is the only way to measure student learning, there will be little incentive toward creating a classroom that uses cooperative learning as a tool for education and for character development.

Research tends to substantiate the value of cooperative learning in the development of both intellectual and social skills. Robert Slavin (1990) writes:

> There is agreement that—at least in elementary and middle/junior high schools and with basic skills objectives—cooperative methods that incorporate group goals and individual accountability accelerate student learning considerably. Further, there is agreement that these methods have positive effects on a wide array of affective outcomes such as inter-group relations, acceptance of mainstreamed students, and self-esteem. (p. 54)

The importance of inter-group relations cannot be overstated. The needs of society demand that individuals of different races and beliefs work together to solve problems. Slavin (1983) and Kagan et al. (1985) noted that an analysis of cooperative education studies indicates that cross-ethnic friendships increased in classes that used cooperative education in relation to control classes that did not. The students involved in cooperative learning were more likely to state that a child from a different racial background was a friend. Cooperative learning can also improve the relationships between academically handicapped students and their more traditional classroom peers (Madden and Slavin, 1983). Cooperative learning provides the opportunity for students to learn academic skills and care about the feelings and needs of others in their groups. It requires that students assume responsibility for themselves and for the success of the group. Cooperative learning, to be successful, requires that students learn to respect the contributions that others bring to the learning environment.

An excellent example of a strong, research-based, cooperative learning program is Cooperative Integrated Reading and Composition, or CIRC, developed at Johns Hopkins University by Professors Madden, Steven, and Slavin. CIRC integrates reading and language arts/writing activities. Students are assigned to reading groups of eight to 15 students. The students within a group are divided into teams of four, which are then divided into pairs. The groups are heterogeneous so that low-level and high-level reading students can be in teams and paired together. Work is done in pairs or in teams. The teacher, who works with the reading groups approximately 20 minutes each day, introduces vocabulary and instructs the students in skills needed to work successfully in teams to accomplish their assigned tasks. The teams use the following sequence in "attacking" the reading.

1. The students pair up and read the story silently, then take turns reading the story aloud. The partner is responsible for assisting if difficulties arise with the reading.
2. Students, halfway through the story, stop reading and identify characters, settings, and predict how the story will end. Students know they will write on an assigned topic after the story is completed.
3. Students are given word lists which feature difficult words from the reading. The students are expected to practice until they master saying the words.
4. Students look up story words in a dictionary, paraphrase the definition and write sentences.
5. Students summarize the main part of the story with their partners. A list of essential story elements allows students to check their summaries.
6. After three class periods of work, students are given a test on the story. They define the story words and must exhibit proficiency on the word lists. The tests are done individually.

The research is quite impressive on CIRC. Students participating in the program showed solid gains in reading comprehension and reading vocabulary compared to students who did not participate. CIRC students also showed solid growth in the writing process compared to students who did not participate in the program. Working cooperatively helped students improve important academic skills. It also allowed them to assume responsibility for themselves and for others. This reflects an environment that more closely models the social skills and character traits needed in life.

Once students are required to work together, to cooperate in achieving goals, they are bound together more than if they just completed their work at their individual desks. Students need to "reach out and touch each other," to put aside individual needs and desires if they are to achieve their goals and the goals we establish for them. Alfie Kohn (1991) fully recognizes that:

> [C]ooperative learning promotes pro-social behavior. Having children learn from one another creates powerful bonds between them and sends a message very different from that sent by a classroom in which each child is on his or her own—or, worse still, one in which the success of each is inversely related to the success of the others....Cooperation is an essentially humanizing experience that predisposes participants to take a benevolent view of others. It allows them to transcend egocentric and objectifying postures and encourages trust, sensitivity, open communication, and pro-social activity. (p. 504)

This being said, one should be careful to plan and structure cooperative learning activities, or one may find that a single individual does all the work for the group. This usually happens because an excellent student can complete the assignment and do a better job than the others, but allowing this to happen is detrimental, for the excellent student as well as the others in the group. The excellent student is unable to recognize that others in the group have talents and skills, and the other group members may fail to practice or apply their own skills. The best cooperative learning activities involve the application of various skills and demonstrate that several minds working together are better than one working alone. (Keep in mind that not every instructional class period needs to involve cooperative work. Students should work individually to master certain skills and knowledge contained within the curriculum.)

David W. Johnson and Roger T. Johnson (1990) wrote that to achieve mutual goals students must develop skills in working together. The skills are:

1. Get to know and trust one another.
2. Communicate accurately and unambiguously.
3. Accept and support one another.
4. Resolve conflicts constructively. (p. 30)

These are the same skills that students must develop to facilitate effective cooperative learning. Johnson and Johnson argue that students must see that a skill is valuable and recognize they would be better off knowing the skill. Brainstorming would be an example of a valuable skill. Properly used, it allows students to generate many possible ideas without immediately evaluating the merit of the ideas.

Second, the students need to understand when a skill should be used. Brainstorming a list of possible options is an unnecessary skill if the goal of the assignment is to evaluate three preset options.

Third, the skill must be practiced again and again. Think back to Chapter 3 and the importance of repeating good practices. To develop procedural skills, one needs to practice and rehearse them. The same applies to learning skills used in cooperative ventures such as brainstorming. For instance, when brainstorming in a group, one individual may be the recorder while three others are free to generate ideas. Each time the group practices brainstorming, a different student should act as recorder so that all experience being a recorder as well as a brainstormer. In this manner, each student is being asked to practice the various skills within the cooperative learning environment.

Fourth, students must process how frequently and how well they are doing the skill. This requires that teachers allow time for students to reflect on their efforts. How well is the group able to brainstorm alternatives? How well do group members build on the ideas of others? Groups should be encouraged to reflect on the skills they are doing well, as well as on the skills they can improve. This reflection should be a positive venture and is essential for groups to improve. After all, if we as adults do not have time to reflect on and evaluate what we are doing, we will not improve. The same applies to students in cooperative groups.

Making Cooperative Education Work

Denise Baxter-Yoder, a fifth grade teacher at Startown Elementary School in Newton, North Carolina, combines elements from various cooperative learning theorists to create a positive cooperative learning exercise. Denise describes a lesson:

> Using the novel *Sarah, Plain and Tall* by Patricia MacLachlan, the students will focus on pages 3-32. Using Kagan's structure, "Think-Pair-Share," students will be asked to respond to a series of prediction questions. In this structure, the first step is "think." Think time is very important because each child has time to silently formulate his/her answer to the question. This allows the more impulsive child to put more thought into his answer and allows the more reticent child a chance to think before he has been influenced by someone else's opinion. Upon completion of the individual thought period, the child signals that he/she is ready for the next step with a thumbs-up gesture. When both partners have given the signal, the students form pairs. Each partner shares his/her idea. They decide to agree, disagree, or augment their thinking. The final step is "share." The partners can share in a variety of ways. They can share their answers orally with the class; they can write their answers on slates; they can write their answers on charts. These are three steps in a very simple but effective structure. Positive interdependence, respect for what each has to offer to achieve the learning goal, is developed because the students are sharing their thoughts, and individual accountability is stressed because students know they will share the information, in some manner, with the class.

Next, three or four questions will be asked in order to stimulate interest prior to the actual reading portion for this lesson. Possible questions might be, "How would your life be different if you lived in the past on a prairie?" and "What kinds of responsibilities would you have if you were the head of a household at the age you are now?" To increase the level of each child's participation, a structure called "Round Robin," designed by Spencer Kagan, is used. The teacher poses a question. The students think of their responses. A signal is given to begin sharing ideas in an ordered rotation around the group. After each person responds orally, the group may then give a signal to the teacher indicating its readiness to share with the class. Notice the importance of what each student brings to the exercise is recognized. Students can build on each other's ideas to develop a greater understanding of the question or issue.

Now the class is ready to move into the reading segment. This portion of the lesson is similar to the CIRC program developed by Slavin. Vocabulary words for the day are placed on the overhead. The students respond chorally after each word is pronounced and highlighted by the teacher. Several sentences, providing contextual clues, are read containing the target vocabulary words. Students are asked to identify the clues that would give meaning to the targeted word. Once again, Think, Pair and Share can be used to increase the participation.

Afterwards, the students read targeted passages silently. This allows each child to gain familiarity with the selection as well as building a "mental rehearsal" for the oral reading that follows. Finally, the students pair and read quietly with heads together and voices lowered for close proximity. This gives all children the opportunity to read and reduces stress levels since the partner is the only one who is hearing the reading.

Baxter-Yoder then moves the class into other cooperative activities. This is truly a wonderful class to observe. The entire class of students works together to achieve both academic and social goals.

There are two keys to this class and any other successful cooperative learning venture. The first is the structure of the lesson. The teacher provides a time period and expects the students to work responsibly within this period. There is little time for slackness! Second, the students know the procedures to be used in class via previous practice and application. The class has practiced Think, Pair and Share over and over in various academic subjects. It's a procedural skill the students have learned well.

The Character Result

By requiring that students work together to accomplish group goals, cooperative learning becomes a valuable tool in the development of character. Students develop individual responsibility as well as responsibility toward the group goals. Cooperative learning activities enable students to recognize the various gifts that others bring to a learning environment. Finally, cooperative learning offers students the opportunity to further develop and practice caring toward their peers. All this can be accomplished without diminishing the academic development of students.

Perhaps no organization has worked with greater emphasis on the use of cooperative learning than the Developmental Studies Center (DSC) in San Ramon, California. There students are recognized as having intrinsic motivation to learn and to fit into their social groups. Thus, emphasis is made on the importance of cooperative learning both for intellectual and social pursuits. The DSC has organized lessons in an excellent book, *Blueprints for a Collaborative Classroom* (1997), with the following considerations about how children learn:

CHILDREN'S SOCIAL DEVELOPMENT AND ACADEMIC GROWTH ARE INTERTWINED AND ARE BEST FOSTERED IN INTERACTIVE LEARNING SITUATIONS—Social growth and intellectual development occur together—not always at the same moment, but certainly hand in hand.

CHILDREN NEED ASSISTANCE LEARNING HOW TO APPLY VALUES IN DAILY LIFE—This may require modeling and role-playing particular strategies, as well as seeking social and academic reflection at the end of the activity.

CHILDREN NEED "HANDS-ON" PRACTICE TO DEVELOP CONCEPTUAL UNDERSTANDING—Collaborating with classmates helps students understand abstract concepts such as fairness and responsibility.

CHILDREN NEED TO FEEL A MEASURE OF CONTROL OVER THEIR LEARNING—They need to explore knowledge and ideas, to practice making good choices, and to take responsibility for their learning.

CHILDREN LEARN BEST WHEN PRESENTED WITH CHALLENGES THAT ARE NEITHER TOO EASY NOR TOO DIFFICULT—Learning can be addressed in more than one way, leaving children choices about the form and content of their work.

CHILDREN ARE MORE WILLING TO TAKE ON CHALLENGING TASKS IN A SUPPORTIVE ENVIRONMENT—They want to anticipate and analyze their successes and problems in ways that create supportive groups and a supportive classroom.

CHILDREN ARE NATURALLY MOTIVATED TO LEARN ABOUT TOPICS THEY CONSIDER IMPORTANT, RELEVANT, OR FUN—Short-term goals of an activity can contribute to the broader academic goals and social norms of the class.

CHILDREN ARE MORE LIKELY TO INTERNALIZE LEARNING WHEN THEY REFLECT ON WHAT AND HOW THEY LEARNED—The act of expressing what they have learned, or of hearing it in a new way from a classmate, often deepens students' understanding and helps them make the new learning their own. (pp. 6-7)

According to the DSC, as a cooperative learning facilitator (i.e., teacher) you must prepare the children for the activity by posting and reviewing the how-to directions so students know the steps needed to be successful. To be successful in the group work, the students may need to practice the steps involved in the activity. The facilitator must recognize that not all students will be successful immediately but refrain from intervening too soon to let the group work its way through the difficulty. This is very important. The goal is for the group to do the work and complete its task alone. Struggle and problem solving is not necessarily detrimental to learning. Indeed, I believe it facilitates learning. When the teacher notes a group struggling, not making progress, and feeling frustration and perhaps anger, intervention via questioning and dialogue to help the process are needed. In North Carolina there is an old saying, "Cold weather makes good timber." However constant freezing weather may hurt the trees. The facilitator must determine if the weather is cold or freezing!

Finally the students must reflect what they have learned academically as well as socially. The DSC also recognizes that children with little collaborative experience may need to work in pairs before moving to larger group work. They also recommend that the cooperative learning groups never have more than four members. As the students become more socially and academically skillful in their efforts, the grouping can change from random or a constant rotating of members within groups to groups that are teacher selected or groups that have particular interests in topics they would like to pursue. I would urge anyone who is serious about using cooperative learning as a tool for social and academic development to seek out the materials and insights provided by the Developmental Studies Center.

What can we infer from Baxter-Yoder's practical experience, as well as the research of organizations such as the DSC? First, schools could consider entire staff training on how to use cooperative education in their curriculums. The preparation of a cooperative learning activity requires *structure* and *organization*, which require training. Any organization seeking to change the way "business is done" must train its employees in the new procedures.

The organization must also give employees time and opportunity to practice the skills by working together until they reach competency. The same applies to schools. All teachers on staff will benefit from receiving training in how to implement cooperative learning as a vital part of the academic and social environment of the school. Teachers can plan together and develop lesson plans when cooperative learning can be used to facilitate the academic and social goals. When the teacher/facilitator begins more intentional cooperative learning activities, a request for peer observations can be helpful. Peers can come into the class to observe how the facilitator/teacher is working with the groups. Is the teacher providing enough structure? Is the teacher moving into groups too quickly if a group is struggling? Often another's eyes can be better than those of the one immediately engaged. Finally, teachers should try to do a brief, written narrative after the lesson as a means of reflection. I have found it helpful to ask a few simple questions: What was the goal(s) of the lesson? Were we successful? What were some strengths? What would I like to improve?

Teachers will model and remind students of the character traits of responsibility for individual and group achievement, and respect for others in the group. The application of these character traits is needed to complete the group exercise successfully. Remember, although it's not necessary to use cooperative learning in every class period, all students should develop this skill. Students must also receive training in the procedures of cooperative learning before they can successfully demonstrate this skill. It may be helpful to post procedures on the wall to remind students of the steps and procedures needed for cooperative learning. In general, cooperative groups should be heterogeneously grouped. Depending on the nature of the assignment, there could also be times when academically talented students work together in a cooperative venture. To encourage interest and excitement among the students for more of this kind of work, cooperative learning should be celebrated. Post examples of group work on walls. What is valued is learned.

Teachers must also be patient with students as they learn to work cooperatively. The maxim "Anything worth doing well is worth doing poorly!" should act as a guideline. If something is of merit, we must be patient and recognize that individuals might perform the task poorly at first but will improve if given enough time and frequent practice opportunities. The payoff will be students who master the curriculum and develop virtues such as being respectful of the efforts of others and fully responsible for their part of the task. Think back to Siecor's cooperative work environments at the beginning of the chapter. The great success Siecor has realized depends on having people work together in teams to solve problems. The teams are successful because each person is important to the team success and works hard for it. Only through this type of cooperation can Siecor's teams—and thus Siecor itself—continue to be successful. The same applies to our schools. When we teach students to work cooperatively—being respectful to others and responsible for themselves as contributors—our schools will become places where students learn and work together. What could be better preparation for their future? Cooperative learning in school has a critical role in developing character in our children!

Chapter 5

Teaching for Thinking

What separated our primitive ancestors from the creatures they ate was primarily their capacity for thinking beyond mere survival. We even have, on the walls of caves, some 10,000-year-old expressions of their individuality in art and storytelling. The foundation of civilization has its roots set firmly in the development and expansion of reason. Our current concept of thinking sprang up among a small group of men only 2,300 years ago in Greece. They sought to develop consistency and accuracy of thought based upon the development of logic and reason. These individuals were called philosophers, and their mental "craft" was called philosophy.

Originally defined as the "study of wisdom," philosophy is first a *re*thinking operation. Rethinking is considering what one has thought with the addition of more information. This is an important concept. In the physical sciences and the humanities, the fundamental principle of objectivity is that of rethinking, or reconsideration. That is, to be objective, one ought to be willing to reconsider the underlying beliefs and assumptions that support the behaviors indigenous to one's way of life. Why is this so? A rethinking operation allows us to consider and reconsider the ideas of others. Might their insights help us in our work? Might the act of rethinking force us to reassess our assumptions and therefore grow in knowledge and wisdom? This can be achieved through the work of the solitary scholar or through the collaborative efforts of a team or like-minded individuals.

History is replete with acts of rethinking. Galileo rethought the way the planets moved around the sun. Physicians were sure blood pumped out and back to the heart through the same vessels until William Harvey rethought the model and discovered blood circulation. Albert Einstein rethought the concepts of space and time; Niels Bohr, Werner Heisenberg, James Chadwick, and Enrico Fermi rethought the atom and helped give us a new paradigm for the subatomic world. Cubist painters Jena Metzinger and Pablo Picasso redefined our concept of art. I could go on and on. What is important is that each of these individuals reconsidered previous assumptions and opened up a new world—into which new thinkers immediately headed. If a person is unwilling to think and rethink the raw data of experience or the sources of such data when new information is discovered, there can be no basis for comparison when conflict and inconsistencies occur. All the notable people mentioned—plus all the many people who act to improve the daily lives of others—are willing to think and rethink.

Often in seminars or guided discussions, students recognize the inconsistencies of their stated positions. I've had students, when discussing "The Mending Wall" by Robert Frost, rethink their opinions of Frost's neighbor—that perhaps the function of ritual, mending the wall, is important even if the wall no longer serves any practical purpose. The child learns to think, listen to others, and see if their insights provide a greater or more complete understanding. Wouldn't you like to think children are doing that throughout their day?

Philosophy is also about understanding concepts. Concepts, more general than facts, help organize particular events, attributes, or facts into meaningful categories. "Justice," "fairness," and "nation" are concepts—abstractions that are used to organize current experiences and information and to provide commonality to old ones. For example, once a huge nation, the former Soviet Union has been broken into many new, smaller nations, yet the concept "nation" has not changed in our minds. The concept gives us the idea that each of those new nations has elements (such as a central government and legal boundaries) found in all nations. The concept of nation organizes for us the particulars of nationhood. The same could be said for the concept "justice." The particulars of justice might vary from state to state or nation to nation, yet the concept of justice is stable, meaning an attempt to treat individuals in a fair, consistent manner.

One of the major functions of education is to develop in students the ability to think clearly and consistently, to enable students to think and rethink regarding their ideas and perspectives. The philosophical life reflects this quality. The habit of thinking about ideas and experiences, as opposed to simply acting on impulse or letting the mind wander during inactive moments, is evidence that a person, no matter what age, has taken up the philosophical or thinking life.

As educators and parents, one of our goals is insuring that our students possess the ability to think and reason, to make judgments and wise choices, to figure out situations they've never encountered before, to think beyond themselves and their immediate desires, and to engage in the philosophical life. It's also one of the easiest for us to achieve. Children are naturally inquisitive and are continually seeking to find meaning in adults' behavior, to develop some consistent "theory of ethics." They readily move to discussions of right and wrong although they may not be consistent in their philosophical or ethical assertions. As educators, we must recognize that it's not enough simply to discuss a personal view of what is right or wrong, good or evil. Values clarification taught us the folly of this. We must be pro-active to help students formulate standards or concepts that will help them in all their pursuits in life. We must help them become philosophers. This will demand that teachers model what we wish our students to do. If we want students who think and contemplate, then we must think and contemplate. Lawrence Kohlberg's warning to us must be heeded, "[I]f the child is a moral philosopher, then the teacher must be also."

Why should we be concerned about teaching for thinking if our interest is in character development? Let's go back to the ancient Greeks. When we more closely examine the function of reason in ancient Greece, we discover it was directly connected to making sound moral judgments. Aristotle felt that the good person is nurtured through the development of good habits (i.e., rules and procedures), as well as the development of the intellect—the ability to think and reflect on determining the proper ethical course of action. In this account he was, of course, following in the footsteps of his teacher, Plato. The practice of thinking then helps develop the ethical awareness of the person.

To know what is good, or what is meaningful or beautiful, we must engage in a process of comparing and contrasting ideas to understand better the perspective of the author, speaker, or artist. When we are thoughtfully engaged in a serious conversation, we are assessing what is stated, relating this to our own experiences, and then determining if we agree or disagree with the statement. Our desire and ability to agree and disagree, and to frame a solid, consistent argument are based on our ability and disposition to think and reason. The development of reason and clear thinking is also helpful when novel situations demand a thoughtful action, not simply a response based on habit. To know the good, one must be able to think and reflect, to apply the skills of thinking.

Thinking Skills

Robert Ennis defines critical thinking as "reasonable and reflective thinking that is focused on deciding what to believe and do." He maintains that "genuine reflective thinking" requires premises of an ethical nature. Without these ethical principles, critical thinking can serve the closed-minded or the open-minded thinker equally well. But those with genuine open-mindedness, Ennis claims, will (a) seriously consider points of view other than their own, (b) reason from premises with which they may disagree without letting their disagreement interfere with their reasons, and (c) withhold judgment when the evidence and reasons are insufficient.

Ennis provides directives for those who engage in critical thinking. I find it difficult to distinguish "critical thinking" from "good thinking," so I consider his list, below, directives for good thinkers.

1. Seek a clear statement of the thesis or question.
2. Seek reasons.
3. Try to be well informed.
4. Use credible sources and mention them.
5. Take into account the total situation.
6. Try to remain relevant to the main point.
7. Keep in mind the original and/or basic concern.
8. Look for alternatives.
9. Be open-minded.
    a) Consider seriously other points of view than one's own (dialogical thinking).
    b) Reason from premises with which one disagrees—without letting the disagreement interfere with one's reasoning.
    c) Withhold judgment when the evidence and reasons are insufficient.

10. Take a position (and change a position) when the evidence and reasons are sufficient to do so.
11. Seek as much precision as the subject permits.
12. Deal in an orderly manner with the parts of a complex whole.
13. Be disposed to use the listed critical thinking abilities.
14. Be sensitive to the feelings, level of knowledge, and degree of sophistication of others.

These are the approaches of thoughtful persons. To encourage the development of these attitudes, schools must become centers where serious thinking is expected. To accomplish this goal, schools will need to treat critical thinking as a skill that can be taught, learned, and applied to issues of ethical, moral, and social significance.

To learn to think and rethink, students must learn to be disciplined in their methodology. They must learn skills and when to apply those skills. For example, when students study various characters from literature, they may apply the skill of comparing and contrasting, but may not need to use the skill of brainstorming. Second, there is a sequence in learning thinking skills. One must practice the skill of sequencing before one is able to apply the skill of recognizing cause and effect. To use an analogy from baseball, one must be able to catch and throw the ball before one can execute a double play. Third, in thinking one may need to apply ethical reasoning, especially if one is determining obligations owed to others. For example, assessing ideas contained within Dr. Martin Luther King, Jr.'s "Letter From Birmingham City Jail" requires that we take into account the social and moral demands of the piece.

Critical thinking demands we be logical, but it also demands we use our moral sense and be ethically consistent in our pronouncements. If we want students to think critically, we must help them learn to think logically and ethically. There are two particular instructional approaches that can be used to facilitate students' thinking: Mortimer Adler's Paideia Program and the graphic organizers developed by Joseph P. Hester in his program, Teaching for Thinking.

Paideia Program

It's important not to separate teaching for thinking from the general curriculum. Programs that try to teach thinking skills apart from the curriculum run the risk of having students unable to transfer the skills to the immediate task of mastering a standard course of study. One program that successfully integrates thinking skills and curriculum content is the Paideia Program spearheaded by the noted philosopher Mortimer Adler and described in his *The Paideia Program* (1984). The main goal of the Paideia Program is

> as an educational manifesto calling for a radical reform of basic school-ing in the United States to overcome the elitism of our school system from its beginning to the present day, and to replace it with a truly democratic system that aims not only to improve the quality of basic schooling in this country, but also aims to make that quality accessible to all our children. (p. 1)

Below is a graphic representation of the Paideia Proposal.

STRANDS OF THE PAIDEIA PROPOSAL

	Column One	Column Two	Column Three
GOALS	Acquisition of organized knowledge	Development of intellectual skills & the skills of learning	Enlarged understand-ing of ideas & values
MEANS	**By means of...** Didactic instruction lectures & response	**By means of...** Coaching, exercises, & supervised practice	**By means of...** Maieutic or Socratic questioning and active participation
AREAS Operations Activities	**In three areas of subject matter...** Language, literature & the fine arts Mathematics & natural science History, geography & social studies	**In the operation of...** Reading, writing, speaking, listening Calculating problem solving, observing, measuring Estimating, exercising critical judgment	**In the...** Discussion of books, works of art, and involvement in artistic activities such as drama, music, and the visual arts. (Adler 1984, p. 8)

Each column needs some additional explanation. Column One reflects what is to be taught. Students need to acquire knowledge, information from lectures, films, and question and answers. All the traditional academic areas are to be studied. The focus is on helping the students acquire and organize information.

Column Two reflects the focus on the development of intellectual skills and the skills needed to extend learning. Some of these skills are analysis, synthesis, and evaluation. This is the most difficult aspect of the program. Teachers must work with students to help them develop the skills by which they'll gain a greater understanding of what authors and thinkers mean by their assertions. The teaching of Column Two skills allows students to reflect on the whys and hows, for one must be able to speak and listen to others and exercise critical judgment to understand what an author is trying to share. It is at this point that the teaching of skills to students must be emphasized and checked for mastery. This requires that a teacher work with small groups and with individual students to insure that they are applying and mastering the needed skills.

Column Three, the seminar, represents the application of the skills learned in Column Two. In the seminar, students discuss books, chapters, and artistic works. They do not use or discuss summaries provided in textbooks. The reason for this is that textbooks, unless they are anthologies, generally do not provide enough ideas or insights to have a successful discussion. They are fine for providing broad overviews but do little toward helping students develop a greater understanding of issues. Column Three is designed to help students gain a greater understanding of issues and ideas through the guidance of a leader and the shared ideas of members of the class. Seminars demand rigorous thinking and the sharing of ideas. The goal is to create a greater understanding of the important ideas and concepts within the text. For example, in a seminar discussion, students could analyze the strength or weakness of an argument concerning justice or fairness. This is where the teaching of skills in Column Two pays off. As students learn to apply skills, they develop a better understanding of various issues within the subject area. However, this does not mean they can master the meaning of the material on their own. They need to share their ideas and listen to the ideas of others to gain a greater understanding. In this manner, reflection of what is good and proper is provided in an environment that emphasizes clear thinking. It is not simply a sharing session, but a time to reflect and consider difficult issues and ideas.

Theodore Sizer, writing in Adler's *Paideia Program* (1984), says:

> Central to this brief vignette is the focus on the student's doing—thinking and expressing the results of thought. The teacher acted only as a coach. He helped the students mold their thinking skills and their habits of intellectual inquiry. Such skill training is the backbone of basic schooling. It proceeds one by one, each student gaining skill through critiqued experience. Schools that make this possible are effective schools.

The Paideia Proposal merits serious consideration by those who value the development of thinking and reasoning skills for students. The application of the program requires a rethinking of what occurs in traditional schools. However, the development of thinking skills through Column Two, in preparation for discussion of writings and art, also deserves serious consideration for any school wishing to infuse critical thinking into the curriculum.

Graphic Organizers

Good teachers know that students learn better when a variety of learning styles are taken into account. For example, some students are visual learners. They need to see what is being discussed. Others are auditory learners. It is not enough for them to read notes off the blackboard; they need to hear the teacher discuss the notes. Still others are kinesthetics—they need to write, draw, or make notes in order to understand a particular concept.

The majority of us find it easiest if we are able to make notes or present our thinking in a visual manner. Often, making notes or trying to illustrate what is being said helps us "see" what the speaker is saying. The same method is useful if we are trying to clarify some of our own ideas. A tool to help many individuals graph their learning is a thinking or graphic organizer. These graphic organizers, or maps, come in many different styles and types, but they all have in common a scheme which allows students to organize their thinking.

Joseph P. Hester's research demonstrates that "thinking" is appropriately a "problem-solving process." As such, all thinking begins when a person feels uneasy about something: Maybe some information is missing; maybe a person has been put in an intellectually confusing position. Whatever may be the actual case, the person's mind goes to work trying to solve the puzzle or fill in the missing information. Serious thinking is triggered by problems as they present themselves in the daily routine of living.

If you agree with this definition of thinking, then following how Hester developed his own thinking-skill model will be easy. Here are the steps:

1st Define thinking as problem solving (or decision making, which is essentially the same).

2nd Design a visual organizer that mirrors the steps of problem solving. Problem solving is basically a six-step procedure:

1. Identify the problem to be solved or situation requiring a decision to be made.
2. List all options (this could require some research).
3. List the consequences of each option under consideration. Support the selection of consequences with facts.
4. Assess each option by evaluating its consequences. Establish criteria for saying that a consequence is good or bad. Is the consequence supported by factual information? Is it relevant to the option under consideration that potentially can solve the problem?
5. Assess the consequences by ethical criteria such as: Is the consequence fair to all involved with the situation? Will it cause more harm than good?
6. After considering options and assessing all consequences, select one option and state the reasons for selecting it.

3rd After the problem-solving process has been carefully defined, focus on the micro-thinking skills necessary to be an efficient problem solver.

The visual organizer that defines the problem-solving process will look something like this:

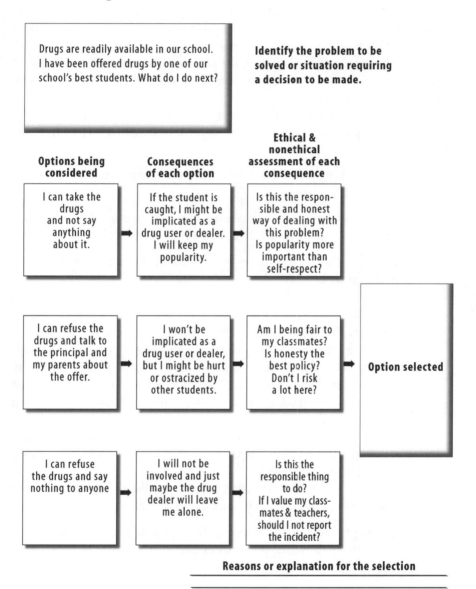

Drugs are readily available in our school. I have been offered drugs by one of our school's best students. What do I do next?

Identify the problem to be solved or situation requiring a decision to be made.

Options being considered

Consequences of each option

Ethical & nonethical assessment of each consequence

I can take the drugs and not say anything about it.

If the student is caught, I might be implicated as a drug user or dealer. I will keep my popularity.

Is this the respon-sible and honest way of dealing with this problem? Is popularity more important than self-respect?

I can refuse the drugs and talk to the principal and my parents about the offer.

I won't be implicated as a drug user or dealer, but I might be hurt or ostracized by other students.

Am I being fair to my classmates? Is honesty the best policy? Don't I risk a lot here?

Option selected

I can refuse the drugs and say nothing to anyone

I will not be involved and just maybe the drug dealer will leave me alone.

Is this the responsible thing to do? If I value my class-mates & teachers, should I not report the incident?

Reasons or explanation for the selection

Hester's organizer helps a student consider the options and consequences, as well as ethical and non-ethical assessments of each proposed option and consequence. Notice how much richer this is than just asking students what they would do in a situation. This requires students to consider the ethical consequences of their decisions. The visual organizer mirrors the skill of problem solving and helps students graphically organize their ideas, options, and evaluations. Then they can proceed to the third step in Hester's thinking-skill model, the development of micro-thinking skills.

In his research, Hester discovered six basic thinking skills that adequately support the problem-solving process. These skills include, but aren't limited to, the following:

1. DEFINING. We define words, concepts, and other important terms in the contexts in which they occur. Associated with this skill are describing and brainstorming. The first step in the problem-solving process is being able to define the problem/ situation. Practicing this skill will help students become better problem solvers. Brainstorming is important as well, for the student will need to think of as many solution-options as possible.

2. SEQUENCING/SERIATING. Being able to organize information in a given order or to prioritize information includes the skills of sequencing and seriating. These are especially necessary in the writing process, but they're also important when evaluating an event or behavior to show the importance (priority) of one behavior over another.

3. CLASSIFICATION. In problem solving, we must classify or group information, such as options and their consequences, in like patterns. This increases our depth of knowledge and under-standing, for we're able to see how pieces of information are related to other pieces. The skill of classification can be used with all ages and levels of students to organize, among other things, ideas, concepts, and characteristics of people.

4. COMPARING/CONTRASTING. Students, to become excellent prob-lem solvers, must master the skill of comparing and contrasting significant likenesses and differences among people, events, and ideas. In the evaluation of consequences and options, and in the choice of a right answer or correct behavior, students must

be able to compare and contrast all the pertinent information they have before them. This skill enables them to develop relationships among different kinds of people, behavior, and ideas for making interpretations or reaching conclusions.

5. CAUSE/EFFECT. In problem solving we want to know what effect some option, if chosen, might have. An effect in this case is nothing more than the consequence of the option that was chosen. Cause/effect relationships are also used in predicting and inferring, which are the heart of hypothesis formation. For example, what will be the consequence of choosing option A over option B? We examine the known facts and from this foundation make an "educated guess," which is nothing more than a prediction, transforming an inference from what we know to something we're not quite sure of, an hypothesis: "Because A is factual or true, then we can safely say (assume) that this other thing, B, is also true because B is consistent with A, doesn't contradict A, and is usually associated with A." In any cause/effect statement, there must be supporting and relevant facts. If we need to, we can employ evaluation at this time to assess the effect as either desirable or undesirable, good or not so good. This can also wait until the problem-solving situation is fully joined.

6. EXPLANATION. Sometimes this skill is called "causal explanation." Think of it as the reverse of cause and effect: You have an event, a behavior, a situation, or a rule to be followed, and you want to know what caused the event, the behavior, the situation, or how to explain it. In problem solving, the student must move forward and backward in selecting the option that is ultimately chosen. Normally we think of options, their consequences, and the facts that support them, and evaluate them by some criteria. We then make our choice, guided by those criteria. But there are situations in which someone does something we think is just awful or something that is wonderful and we say: "Why did he do that?" "What she did was awful!" or "I wouldn't have the courage to do it." Here we are thinking backward, from event to cause, in which case we are seeking the reasons that explain it.

Following are some visual organizers that graphically illustrate each of these skills. They are helpful because they enable students to connect an abstract thinking process to a visual object using a common visual language.

Describing/Brainstorming Visual Organizer

Use this graphic when the class is engaged in a brainstorming activity, or when a concept, idea, person, event, or behavior is in need of defining.

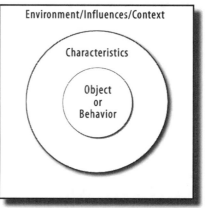

Sequencing Visual Organizer

Use this graphic in the writing process, but it is highly applicable in any sequential activity, especially those requiring ranking or prioritizing options/choices.

For Example: Behaviors I find the most ethical:

Respect	Honesty	Being Fair	Speaking the Truth

Classifying/Organizing Visual Organizer

This graphic can be used to classify simple objects, major ideas, concepts, characteristics of people, behaviors, or events.

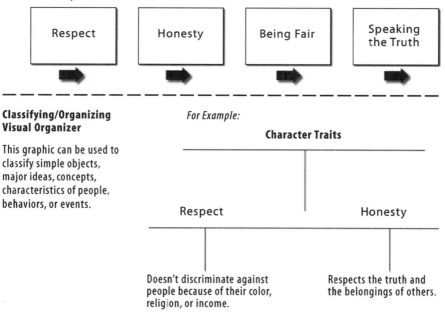

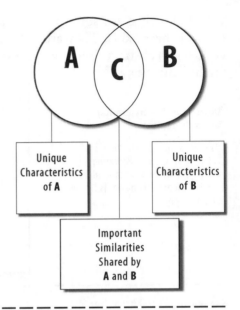

Comparing and Contrasting Visual Organizer

Use this graphic to compare and contrast <u>important</u> likenesses and differences among people, places, things, events, and/or ideas. This tool is useful for developing <u>patterns of relationships</u> among items that are being compared/contrasted for making interpretations and reaching conclusions.

Inferring/Hypothesizing Visual Organizer

Use this graphic to make statements about the unknown (infer) on the basis of the known (hypothesis formation). This skill is used in cause/effect interactions, to predict consequences, and to support observation reports.

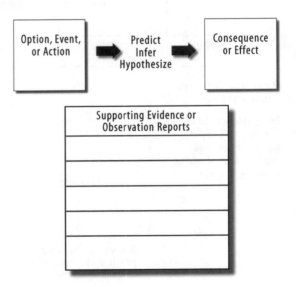

**Explanation of
Visual Organizer**

Use this graphic to assess how well new information supports or explains what else we know or have uncovered through reading, observing, or other kinds of research. Here, the student is being ask to identify some event, action, or behavior (right-hand block) requiring an explanation (left-hand block) and then provide causes, reason, and/or evidence for the event, action, or behavior in question. Here's a helpful hint: This is the same procedure as the skill of inferring effects for causes, but in this case the student knows the effect and is searching for the causes or explanation.

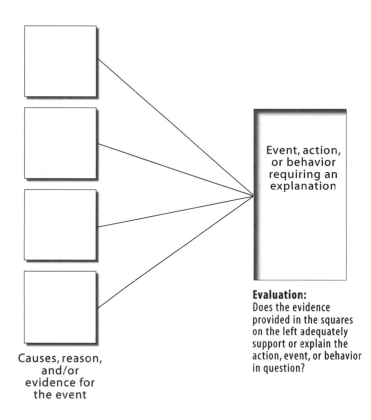

Event, action, or behavior requiring an explanation

Causes, reason, and/or evidence for the event

Evaluation:
Does the evidence provided in the squares on the left adequately support or explain the action, event, or behavior in question?

With the problem-solving process in place, thinking can be integrated into daily lesson planning to help train the minds of students to think thoroughly and efficiently. It's important to use all the appropriate skills—for example, when comparing and contrasting, students should examine significant likenesses and differences. Likewise, it's important that they identify significant patterns and relationships they find while comparing and contrasting.

Using the visual organizers will help students learn complex ideas. They provide a common visual language that guides students through the thinking process; each visual organizer mirrors the skill being used. Visual organizers also hold information in a pattern so students are able to comfortably move back and forth between content and process and the various parts of a problem.

Thinking and Character Connections

Thinking Behaviors	Character Traits	Related Activities
Promoting Interaction	Respecting others by listening	Think-Pair-Share, small group interactions
Thinking About Thinking	Promoting responsibility and honesty	Think logs, journals, and modeling
Promoting Creative Thinking	Trusting and respecting the ideas of others	Encouraging incubation, producing alternatives
Promoting Thinking Visibility	Encouraging honest/responsible use of journals/research	Keeping journals, webbing, and using visual organizers
Promoting Learning Styles	Respecting individual differences	Learning/teaching styles application
Teaching for Transfer	Being responsible in learning and using thinking skills	Applying thinking in all lessons and daily activities
Promoting Thinking Autonomy	Modeling thinking skills and trusting students to apply these skills responsibly	Using responsible problem solving and decision making as a way of life

Apart from providing an ethical problem-solving model, teaching for thinking supports teaching for character development. A person who chooses to be of a high moral character reflects the use of reason in daily decision making, problem solving, and long-range planning. Also, a person who is convinced we should use reason and think through our commitments, obligations, and other daily activities is responsible, respectful, and trustworthy. Teaching for thinking and teaching for character development have compatible goals and mutually supportive outcomes. The classification visual organizer on the previous page will help you "see" the relationship between thinking and character:

Getting Started

How can we learn to improve our students' thinking and thus their ability to reason about what actions and ideas contribute to a good character? First, teachers should develop an understanding of what it means to "teach for thinking." This will require training in various methods and procedures needed to create a thinking classroom. Second, teachers and students working together must identify the thinking skill(s) needed to complete assignments. This will require us—the teachers or parents—to work and continue to work with students to develop the skill(s). Remember the failure of a student to comprehend an assignment and apply the necessary skills is not always the fault of the child. We must seek methods, such as Adler's Paideia or Hester's graphic maps, to help our children and students. Finally, we must create an environment where thinking and the application of thinking is valued—an environment where adults define and children can develop the ability to recognize and reason about ideas, including the ability to recognize and reflect on knowing the good.

Chapter 6

Reading for Character

Dr. John Arnold, retired professor of middle grades education at North Carolina State University, reminded his students on a regular basis that the role of education was to help develop students into good people. Since students don't become good just because someone tells them to be good (any teacher or parent can testify to this!), it behooves us to find every way we can to help them learn good and right behavior.

In this chapter we will consider the role that curriculum and the presentation of the curriculum can play in contributing to the development of good character and ultimately good people. Of special importance is the role literature and narratives play in this process. What children read and how they're taught to read can affect the development of good character traits.

A big bonus for us at the outset is that children have a wonderful love of books. Very young children love to examine picture books and have simple stories read to them. This love of "reading" is often fostered on the lap of a loving relative or in the child's bed before sleep. There are two wonderful consequences when a parent initiates early reading with a child. First, the act of reading and sharing books brings a parent and child closer together. The physical connection promotes an emotional bond that comes with sharing an activity. Second, it lets a child know that reading and discussing books are valued activities, that reading is important and pleasurable, and that it's worth pursuing the satisfaction of reading a good book. The same type of experience occurs in a reading-centered classroom at all educational levels. A teacher can help students develop a love of reading and sharing of ideas. The excitement and educational approach of the teacher encourages students, whether kindergartners or graduate students, to read and share their ideas with others.

Two considerations arise for reading instruction. One is the process of reading. Reading should be taught and enjoyed for its own sake; it will never be a pleasure if it's too difficult to do. To make reading enjoyable for students, we need to develop their reading skills. This can be achieved through a balanced approach of phonics (which acts as a decoder as well), a whole-language approach, which focuses on quality reading, and an immersion into discussion of the reading to create meaning and understanding. The whole-language movement in the United States has helped focus educators on the joy and varied experiences all children bring to the reading/learning process. This movement has forced school districts around the country to assess what their children are reading and to consider the possibility that what one reads and the quality of the reading matters to the child and the teacher.

A second consideration of reading instruction is reading for content and knowledge. In this process we consider what the author is trying to tell us and whether we agree or disagree and why. Reading for content is closely tied to the curriculum. For example, as a high school teacher I might choose some writings by philosophers John Locke, Thomas Hobbes, and Thomas Paine to help students understand the origins of the Declaration of Independence. I may choose some selections from William Faulkner, Carson McCullers, or Walker Percy for an appreciation of the Southern literary tradition. As an elementary teacher, I might have my younger children read Mary Hoffman's *Amazing Grace* or my adolescents Robert Peck's *A Day No Pigs Would Die* to feast on the richness and loveliness of life.

Readings should be chosen to develop in students not only an appreciation of plot and language but also an appreciation of the moral and social issues that discussed in great literature or narratives. Reading becomes a bridge to pass on our cultural traditions and experiences from one generation to another. Our literature and narratives cumulatively help us define and determine our future as well as enlighten us about our past—and not just our distant past. Reading about the recent past that students' parents lived through may prompt discussion at school or home about why people behaved and thought as they did only one generation ago. Children so often tune out anything that begins "When I was your age…" but imagine what conversation might be sparked by a teenager asking, "Dad, we read today about an anti-war protest. Were you ever in a demonstration?"

Literatures and narratives also help us learn and seek to understand the emotions and thoughts of cultures outside our own. Without this bridge we will struggle to gain—or may never gain—an understanding of the ideas and reasoning of others. To help students understand the cultural traditions of others we must seek to grow in ourselves and our students an appreciation of profound writings that include those traditions. For example, Rudyard Kipling's *Captains Courageous* is about a spoiled adolescent boy who learns honor and some cultural tradition from an old Portuguese fisherman.

Profound writing represents literature or narratives that cause us to reflect on the actions, circumstances, and outcomes of individuals and ideas. Great literature and narratives educate us in knowing "what is human about humans." Great readings illuminate human struggles, successes, strengths, weaknesses, virtues, and vices. That's why students have been studying *The Odyssey* for more than 2,000 years, Shakespeare's "Julius Caesar" for 400, *To Kill a Mockingbird* for 40. A study of great ideas set in stories that seem alive to us as readers allows us to gain greater understanding of ourselves.

Great literature comes from throughout the world and is being written on a daily basis—a point I can't stress strongly enough. Any serious literary program that seeks to develop character must include literary classics and contemporary writings from throughout the world.

As educators, we owe our students an exposure to great literature. The primary criterion should be that it is worth reading, not that it's popular for student readers. We have no obligation to teach particular genres of literature, such as adolescent popular fiction, simply because students like to read it. We should use literature identified as adolescent fiction only if the work is worth reading and studying. We should seek to insure that all literature selected for class study tells a wonderful story that prompts a greater understanding of ourselves as humans. One of our jobs as educators is to nurture in children the desire to read great literature and narratives that address our struggling to make sense of our lives and learn the value of the virtues we hold dear, such as being responsible, respectful, kind, courageous, and loyal.

Education should always be geared toward showing students that they can rise above their present mode of thinking and acting and become better persons. William Kilpatrick, Gregory and Suzanne Wolfe wrote in *Books That Build Character* (1994):

> Stories, then, because of their hold on the imagination, can help to create an emotional attachment to goodness. If other things are in place, that emotional attraction can then grow into a real commitment to goodness. The dramatic nature of stories enables us to "rehearse" moral decisions, strengthening our solidarity with the good. (p. 24)

We are not required to have students read what is popular or what speaks to them "where they are." Judy Blume is a popular author for adolescents, but this does not mean that schools should feel obligated to use her writings as part of the literary curriculum. Students can easily read these on their own time.

S. E. Hinton's book, *The Outsiders* (1967) is considered a classic of young adult fiction and has been read by millions of young adults individually and as part of school literature programs. The book, written when Hinton was 16, reflects rebellious youths attempting to find their place in society. The Laurel-Leaf edition describes this book:

> Ponyboy is fourteen, tough and confused, yet sensitive beneath his bold front. Since his parents' deaths, his loyalties have been to his brothers and his gang, the rough, swinging, long-haired boys from the wrong side of the tracks. When his best friend kills a member of a rival gang, a nightmare of violence begins and swiftly envelops Ponyboy in a turbulent chain of events.

Now reflect for a moment. This is a very popular book, and a good teacher could use this book to help students recognize the character growth of Ponyboy. Or to compare and contrast appropriate and inappropriate behaviors. But, simply put, there is much better material for children to read as part of a literary program that has, as one goal, to help develop the character of children. If you're a parent, ask yourself what type of literature you'd like your child to read in a school literary curriculum. I'm not saying that books such as *The Outsiders* are bad to read. They can be quite good for students to read and discuss. But I doubt if many parents and thoughtful educators would want this genre to occupy a large part of a literary curriculum.

It's important that all students learn to read and develop into competent readers. However, what students read assumes considerable importance if we accept that the development of a good character may be facilitated through reading good literature. Educators and parents working together should determine the best and highest quality literature that their children should read. This is not an argument for censorship—it's an issue of selection. Serious or controversial issues should be not avoided. Great literature nearly always addresses issues worth contemplating, so if we guide our students to read quality literature, they will address the issue of character.

Edward Wynne and Kevin Ryan, in *Reclaiming Our Schools* (1993), go further to explain that great narratives, such as fables, philosophy, and religious writings, as well as fiction, can help in the character development of our youth. Students learn from narratives and character-building literature:

- to have both an intellectual and emotional understanding of the lives of good and evil people and what drove them to do what they did.
- to acquire an innate sense of justice and compassion and of greed and cruelty, learned through the study of the narrative's characters.
- to be emotionally touched by some lives and repelled by others.
- to deepen their understanding of and feeling for moral facts of life and ideals continually by seeing them lived out in the narrative's heroes and villains.
- to enhance their moral imagination and moral sensibility as they vicariously experience lives of characters.
- to have greater insight into the lives and stories depicted in literature and history.
- to have a storehouse of moral models to guide them when they act. (p. 156)

So what might be some examples of reading for character? I have chosen examples from four genres that are probably familiar to most adult readers and that can be used by any teacher regardless of curricular assignment. We will examine poems, parables/moral tales, myths, and historical/philosophical writing.

Poetry

First, let us examine the poem "If" by Rudyard Kipling.

If

If you can keep your head when all about you
    Are losing theirs and blaming it on you;
If you can trust yourself when all men doubt you,
    But make allowance for their doubting, too;
If you can wait and not be tired by waiting,
    Or being lied about, don't deal in lies,
Or being hated, don't give way to hating,
    And yet don't look too good, nor talk too wise:
If you can dream—and not make dreams your master;
    If you can think—and not make thoughts your aim,
If you can meet with Triumph and Disaster
    And treat those two impostors just the same;
If you can bear to hear the truth you've spoken
    Twisted by knaves to make a trap for fools,
Or watch the things you gave your life to, broken
    and stoop and build 'em up with worn-out tools:

If you can make one heap of all your winnings
    And risk it on one turn of pitch-and-toss,
And lose, and start again at your beginnings
    And never breathe a word about your loss;
If you can force your heart and nerve and sinew
    to serve your turn long after they are gone,
And so hold on when there is nothing in you
    Except the Will which says to them: 'Hold on!'
If you can talk with crowds and keep your virtue,
    Or walk with Kings—nor lose the common touch,
If neither foes nor loving friends can hurt you,
    If all men count with you but none too much;
If you can fill the unforgiving minute
    With sixty seconds' worth of distance run,
Yours is the earth and everything that's in it,
    And—which is more—you'll be a Man, my son!

Let's forget that Kipling wrote this poem for his son and that it tells his son that if you can do all of this, then "you'll be a Man." Let's change the last line to read, "And—which is more—you'll be a person of character." Would men or women who practiced the mentioned traits be regarded as having good character? Would we desire for our children that they tell the truth, and trust themselves if acting in an honorable manner, to be willing to lose and to start again, and to keep their virtue? If so, then we need to incorporate this poem and poems like this in our literature so that children have time to think about and discuss virtues such as those outlined in the poem.

We can also consider poetry not as famous as Kipling's work. Here are two poems from a wonderful collection titled *The Book of Wisdom*. This simple but powerful poem's author is unknown.

What Cancer Cannot Do

Cancer is so limited—
It cannot cripple love.
It cannot shatter hope.
It cannot corrode faith.
It cannot destroy peace.
It cannot kill friendship.
It cannot suppress memories.
It cannot silence courage.
It cannot invade the soul.
It cannot steal eternal life.
It cannot conquer the spirit.

The following poem by Johann Wolfgang von Goethe could be used with children from all grade levels:

Example

Like the star
Shining afar
Slowly now
And without rest,
Let each man turn, with steady sway,
Round the task that rules the day
And do his best.

Imagine the discussions you could have of only these three poems! All of them cause us to consider that which is excellent and worth emulating. Poetry has a powerful role to play in awakening our moral sense.

Parables

Parable are short, allegorical stories designed to teach some truth or to illustrate a religious principle or moral lesson. They're in story format because people love to hear stories, but they have surprising impact and staying power because they're always true. No listener can refute the truth of a parable, and its message goes deep into the listener's consciousness. It's a good way to get around people's prejudices and preconceptions without confronting them directly.

Jesus often used parables in his teaching because they worked so simply: Present a scenario with a conflict and a resolution whose message often resonates in more than one way. In the New Testament, some of the parables he tells are of the sower reaping what he sows, the prodigal son, and the good Samaritan.

A Zen story tells of a man being chased by a tiger. In running away, he slips over a precipice and is kept from falling to his death by grabbing a tree root. When he looks up he sees the tiger; when he looks down he sees a deep gorge. But at his eye level he sees a ripe strawberry. He plucks and eats it and says, "How delicious is this strawberry now!"

From Buddhist teaching comes a tale of two monks from a sect that forbids touching women. They are walking down a road and come to an enormous puddle, at which a woman is distressed because she cannot get across. Without speaking, one monk picks her up and carries her across, setting her down on the farther edge. The two monks walk on in silence, but an hour later the second monk says, "How could you have broken your vows and touched that woman?" The first monk replies, "Are you still carrying that woman? I put her down an hour ago."

African parables frequently use human behavior attributed to animals as an engaging and effective way to teach right conduct and proper behavior.

The philosopher Christina Hoff Sommers (1992) shares the following widely known tale from a Jewish lesson:

There was once a rabbi in a small Jewish village in Russia who vanished every Friday morning for several hours. The devoted villagers boasted that during these hours their rabbi ascended to Heaven to talk with God. A skeptical newcomer arrived in town, determined to discover where the rabbi really was.

One Friday morning the newcomer hid near the rabbi's house and watched him rise, say his prayers and put on the clothes of a peasant. He saw him take an ax and go into the forest, chop down a tree and gather up a large bundle of wood. Next the rabbi proceeded to a shack in the poorest section of the village in which lived an old woman and her sick son. He left them the wood, which was enough for the week. The rabbi then quietly returned to his own house.

The story concludes that the newcomer stayed on in the village and became a disciple of the rabbi. And whenever he hears one of his fellow villagers say, "On Friday morning our rabbi ascends all the way to heaven." The newcomer quietly adds, "If not higher." (p. 62)

Here is a powerful parable from Aesop about being stubborn for stubborn's sake.

An Oak, which hung over the bank of a river, was blown down by a violent storm of wind, and as it was carried along by the stream, some of its boughs brushed against a Reed which grew near the shore. This struck the Oak with a thought of admiration, and he could not forbear asking the Reed how he came to stand so secure and unhurt, in a tempest which had been furious enough to tear up an oak by the roots? Why, says the Reed, I secure myself by a conduct the reverse of yours: instead of being stubborn and stiff, and confiding in my strength, I yield and bend to the blast, and let it go over me, knowing how vain and fruitless it would be to resist.

Parables, or moral tales, have several advantages for teachers to use in enhancing the character of their students and in teaching us how we should treat others, even those who transgress. Parables are generally short, simple, and easy to understand on the surface, yet they allow for a lot of discussion and contemplation. Even young students would recognize that the rabbi is being very kind to the old woman and her sick son. Parables also offer us a base on which we can build. Teachers can ask students how they might emulate the rabbi or other characters in parables in their family, school, or community. We hope they could put their ideas into action. Parables can play a large role in character education, and it's a clever teacher who can use them effectively.

Myths

Myths help us make sense of the world and offer guidance in the development of character as well. Many students study mythology throughout their literary curriculum. What's important is having the teacher and students discuss what the myths are trying to tell us about acting in a virtuous or just manner, or what they show us about those who are not acting in a just manner. By comparing and contrasting the actions and deeds of various characters, students can come to know and recognize high moral principles. Two excellent examples of character development can be found in *The Aeneid* and *The Odyssey*. Both stories concern the mythological battle of Troy. Aeneas was urged by the gods to flee Troy as the city was falling and take as many people as possible. With a promise from the gods that they would have 10 years of struggle and sacrifice but would eventually have a new homeland, Aeneas led his followers out of the city. After many struggles and challenges, Aeneas and his followers were delivered and founded Rome. Aeneas continued his quest even though he could have stayed with the beautiful queen of Carthage, Dido, and lived a life of luxury. He chose instead to honor his responsibility to his people.

Ulysses simply wanted to return to Greece after the defeat of Troy. In his 20-year journey to get home to his wife and his children, he endured many hardships. Ulysses was even offered the opportunity to become divine by the goddess Calypso if he would stay with her. When he refused, he chose a life of difficulty, but a life of purpose, honor, and love of his family over immortality. He chose responsibility over pleasure. Aren't values such as these worth the attention of students?

Though in American education we're most often exposed to Greek and Roman mythology, a wonderful class project would be to explore mythologies of China, Japan, Scandinavia, Africa, and of Native Americans. They, too, are full of stories of honor and integrity.

Philosophical and Historical Documents

Philosophical and historical documents offer descriptions of the thoughts and actions of mankind. It is crucial that students, especially those at the high school level, read such materials. Far too often, students read history textbooks that offer overviews of historical events or ideas without providing students the opportunity to read actual documents. This kind of teaching is not nearly as effective as it might be. Without reading primary documents, students experience a watered-down view of their heritage. For instance, every high school student should be fully versed in the documents that make up the American "testament": the Declaration of Independence, the Constitution, the Gettysburg Address, and Martin Luther King, Jr.'s "Letter from Birmingham City Jail."

In his powerful piece, King answers a collection of clergymen who have advocated to King, via letter, that he reconsider his actions in Birmingham, Alabama, regarding civil rights. In his reply, King argues why he must continue the protests there, even if some individuals are uncomfortable with the actions of the protesters. He contends that he can justify the breaking of some laws, just as he can argue that other laws should be obeyed. Just laws should be obeyed while unjust laws should not.

> A just law is a man-made code that squares with the moral law or the law of God. An unjust law is a code that is out of harmony with the moral law. To put it in the terms of Saint Thomas Aquinas, an unjust law is a human law that is not rooted in eternal and natural law. Any law that uplifts human personality is just. Any law that degrades human personality is unjust. (King 1991, p. 294)

King states that segregation is wrong because it degrades its victims. He adds that an unjust law such as segregation is one that a majority imposes on a minority but doesn't feel compelled to obey or follow itself. King also challenges the actions of white moderates and churches for their lack of moral response regarding the struggle for civil rights for the African–American. Throughout his writing, King's passion and intellect shine through. It's a powerful lesson on the value of a well-thought-out argument.

Students deserve to read well-crafted works that illustrate human struggles and ideals within a philosophical or historical perspective. They can get excited about the idea that a single document sometimes leads to big changes. Emile Zola's *J'Accuse* was an open letter to the French government challenging its unethical conviction of Captain Dreyfus on spying charges; he eventually was freed. Thomas Paine's Declaration of the Rights of Man, and President Lincoln's Emancipation Proclamation changed the history of America.

Great literature—whether poetry, parable, myth, philosophical/historical writings, or resonant fiction—is characterized by its appeal to both our emotional and intellectual/moral sensibilities. We are moved by the choices of Aeneas and Ulysses. We can admire their character and hope, if we were in their situations, that we would follow in their footsteps. Reading "Letter from Birmingham City Jail," one is touched by King's carefully crafted arguments and also the emotional outrage within the piece. Set in a difficult time in American history, when the philosophical right clashed with cultural demands, the argument appeals to our moral sensibilities. Couldn't a biography about Mother Teresa create similar emotional and intellectual experiences? What about readings from the Bible, or John Steinbeck's *Grapes of Wrath,* or the classic Chinese work *Dream of the Red Chamber,* or Gloria Houston's wonderful book *The Year of the Perfect Christmas Tree,* in which she describes the sacrifices, hopes, and love of a family during World War I?

How to Choose Good Literature

The issue is not whether enough such literature exists. It does, and continues to be written, although contemporary examples may be difficult to find because good literature is not automatically popular. The issue is how we would go about determining literature that is focused on character and have students experience such literature as the bulk of their literary program.

As a start, we could list the various traits of a person of good character as a checklist to help us choose literature and readings for our students/children. Then we can select material in which the characters overcome difficulties (it wouldn't be interesting without conflict!) through right action and by demonstrating traits such as responsibility, perseverance, honesty, and respect.

Before continuing, however, we must recognize that to develop students' rational, moral sensibilities through literature, the literature must be taught! Children must learn and practice intellectual skills (as noted in Chapter 5, Teaching for Thinking) that can be applied to great literature. Two practices I believe have merit in facilitating the moral reasoning ability of students. First, students must be encouraged to talk about the piece, with the goal being to develop greater awareness of the issues in the reading. This requires that we be aware of the developmental thinking of students and set the discussion at the appropriate level for their intellectual experiences and capabilities. Young children are capable of thinking and reflecting on issues and ideas, but they are limited in the ways they express ideas. The pedagogical approaches advocated within the Paideia Program or the Junior Great Books Program offer instructional insights needed to facilitate this process.

Second, students in middle and high school should be expected to keep journals that reflect their personal reactions to the ideas discussed and learned in their readings. The teacher should, on occasion, read the journals and provide feedback to the students, with the goal being to help students think about the issues raised in the journal in a more complete and inclusive manner. Students expressing a point of view limited to self-interest should be urged to consider the needs of others. Again, this type of reflection must consider the developmental and intellectual abilities of the student, but feedback on journal writings can facilitate expanding a student's point of view. The combination of discussion and journal writing helps a student develop the skills and attitudes needed to more fully consider the moral and social issues found in literature and in life. Following are descriptions of three programs that could play a role in a quality literature program.

The Junior Great Books Program

Though not all discussions need to center around issues of character, most eventually do. Great literature revolves around human beings and their struggle to define what is human about humans. This often involves discussing our needs and our wants—which are not necessarily the same! The quality of the literary selections in the Junior Great Books Program provides the opportunity for such discussions. There are four criteria that guide the selection of readings used in the Junior Great Books program:

- First and most important, selections must be able to support extended interpretive discussion. Because students in Great Books programs participate in a collaborative search for meaning in a work, selections must invite and support a number of interpretations.

- Selections must raise genuine questions for adults as well as students. Providing selections that speak to both leaders and students helps ensure that shared-inquiry discussions will be a collaborative effort.

- Selections must be limited in length so that students can read each selection at least twice and work with it closely. Through concentrated work on a single text over a period of several days, students in Great Books programs learn how to read closely—to examine details and draw connections—always with the purpose of working out answers to substantial questions of interpretations.

- Selections must be age-appropriate. When deciding in which series to place a selection, we [The Great Books Foundation] give primary consideration to the appropriateness of its theme and style for a particular grade, rather than to standard assessments of reading levels. In all of the Great Books programs, including the Read-Aloud program, students read or hear aloud the original works of the author: no texts have been modified to meet a controlled vocabulary. (Great Books Foundation, 1992)

The Junior Great Books Program is K-12 in scope. Selections for early primary years are read aloud to the class by the teacher. Much of the material is drawn from folk tales around the world. Some selections are poems from such diverse writers as William Shakespeare and Langston Hughes. For second through twelfth grade, selections are read by the students themselves. The stories, taken from throughout the world, include works by Beatrix Potter, Maya Angelou, Aristotle, Immanuel Kant, and Charles Dickens. All readings have something to teach about the development and application of a good character. The objective of the Junior Great Books Program is to have students engage in shared inquiry with other students via the introduction and discussion of interpretative and evaluative questions that guide the shared inquiry.

Teaching students how to read and how to think—preparing them to be informed and responsible citizens—should be the goal of all American schools. The Junior Great Books curriculum is an innovative, excellent program of interpretive reading, writing, and discussion dedicated to achieving this goal. The curriculum is predicated on the conviction that all students can think critically and derive insight and pleasure from outstanding works of literature. Using the shared-inquiry method of learning, which was developed by the foundation, students work independently and collaboratively to explore divergent possibilities for meaning in rich, challenging texts. (Great Books Foundation, 1992)

The key terms are "interpretive" and "shared inquiry." Both hinge on asking students interpretive questions. Interpretive questions are designed to suggest more than one plausible answer to an issue within the text, requiring the students to support their opinions based on the events within the text. Just because a student has an answer doesn't mean that the answer can be supported by appealing to the text.

For example, take the story "Jack and the Beanstalk." In the Junior Great Books version (there are many versions of this story), Jack is sent by his mother to sell the cow, Milky White. Jack sells the cow for some magic beans and his mother, without providing him supper, sends him to bed with a negative assessment of his intellectual abilities! Jack awakens to discover a beanstalk outside his window. He climbs the beanstalk and meets the ogre's wife. He befriends her, and she hides him from the ogre when he returns to the house. While the ogre is sleeping, Jack makes off with a bag of gold. He returns and shares the gold with his mother. Afterwards, Jack decides to venture back up the beanstalk. He again befriends the ogre's wife, who hides him again. This time Jack escapes with the goose that lays a golden egg. Once again, after a period of time, Jack decides to go back up the beanstalk. This time Jack hides in the house without the wife's help. Both the wife and the ogre sense that he is there and try to find him. They fail and Jack steals the ogre's golden harp. However, the harp sounds an alarm. The ogre awakes from his slumber and begins to chase Jack, who races with the harp down the beanstalk. He calls to his mother who brings him an ax, which he uses to chop down the beanstalk, causing the ogre's death.

Students, after working individually or in small groups over several days, are brought together for "shared inquiry." The discussion of the reading via shared inquiry requires that the students of the class form a circle or semicircle. Through the use of interpretive questions, the leader/teacher initiates a group discussion and sharing of ideas within the story. "Is Jack's good fortune more the result of skill or luck?" is an interpretive question. It requires that students discuss what is meant by luck and skill. It also requires that students refer to the reading to support their ideas. For example, Jack is skillful based on his ability to climb the beanstalk and befriend the ogre's wife. He may be considered lucky that he hides well when the ogre and his wife are looking for him. Interpretive questions help students develop intellectual patience and the habit of taking time to think carefully about serious literature. "Is Jack a good boy?" represents an evaluative question and should be asked only after a thorough interpretive discussion of the text. Stories rich in ideas force students to analyze and develop a greater understanding of actions, ideas, and motives. I have found that a discussion about whether Jack was a good boy can engage adults as well as students in an ethical analysis of Jack's behavior. In all cases, we are left with a greater understanding of what it means or does not mean to be good. In this manner, the habit of serious inquiry is reinforced by the discussion and insights one develops concerning profound ideas.

The Junior Great Books approach has several advantages. The focus of the program, to develop reflective, thinking students through reading good literature, has the potential to facilitate the development of character in students through the intellectual pursuit of meaningful ideas. Students are expected to give serious thought to the selections and be prepared to exchange ideas during the discussions. Students learn to think and rethink their ideas and assumptions as the ideas of others are shared within the group. Luckily, this is a skill that students can learn easily and enjoy.

The program is designed for heterogeneously grouped classes. I have been leading seminars or inquiries for many years and have learned never to underestimate the insights and depth of my students no matter what their IQ! Insights into human character and aspirations are found in all levels of intellectual assessment. The approach demands that students engage in intellectual activity, and intellectual exchange is exciting for both adults and children. I've seen students, when they are engaged in a difficult question or issue, slide to the edge of their seats and hang onto every word being said by their peers. They in turn are ready to agree or disagree, based not on emotions, but on interpretations from the reading of the story. There is nothing more exciting than seeing a student reconsider his or her view of an issue and acknowledge that another's interpretation makes more sense. I have often remarked to other teachers that my understanding of a reading increases every time I lead an inquiry, even if I have discussed a piece many times.

Center for Learning: A Values-Based Reading Program

The idea behind the Center for Learning's Values-Based Reading Program is to "incorporate universal values with academic material that encourages students to grow as vital and caring members of our multicultural society." The Center for Learning, in Rocky River, Ohio, considers the following to be universal ethical values, "crucial for improving the moral climate of our country and the moral muscle of our students":

ADAPTABILITY	FAMILY COMMITMENT	RESPECT
CITIZENSHIP	FREEDOM	RESPONSIBILITY
COMPASSION	GRATITUDE	SELF-ACTUALIZATION
CONSIDERATION	INITIATIVE	SELF-DISCIPLINE
COURAGE	INTEGRITY	SERVICE
DILIGENCE	JUSTICE	TEAMWORK
ENDURANCE	LOYALTY	TRUTH
EQUALITY	PEACE	
FAITH	PRIVACY	

The Center has developed units based on great works of literature, which educators can use to teach and reinforce certain core values. A core directory summarizes the curriculum unity. The following four examples are commonly read books. For each, the center lists themes/cultural setting, ethical values, and academic activities.

THEMES/ CULTURAL SETTING	ETHICAL VALUES	ACADEMIC ACTIVITIES
Across Five Aprils *by Irene Hunt*		
Parallels division in border state during Civil War; reflects family frailties and growing up against background of political upheaval	Compassion Family commitment Integrity Responsibility	Civil War research; debate; interpretive questions; map study; literary analysis; dialectic study...
Antigone *by Sophocles*		
5th-century B.C. Greek tragedy known through translation reflective of Greek belief in oracles and curses; teaches that all choices have consequences and that laws must be just and reasonable	Citizenship Endurance Family commitment Freedom Justice Truth	Comparative study of literary works... character study... analysis of irony and origin of tragedy elements
A Day No Pigs Would Die *by Robert Peck*		
Fictional biography set in late 1920s on Vermont farm; creates vivid atmosphere of Shaker way of life and 12-year-old narrator's struggle to understand his heritage and future responsibilities	Compassion Endurance Faith Integrity Justice Respect Responsibility Self-discipline	...critique of content; reading aloud; character description; comprehension of themes

---

The Witch of Blackbird Pond *by Elizabeth G. Speare*

Portrays life in 17th-century New England colonies; uses themes of social conflict; religious intolerance, superstition….	Compassion Family commitment Loyalty Respect	Development of critical thinking skills…study of characterization… creation of images

---

There are 160 titles available from the Center for Learning, along with extensive activities designed to engage students in thinking and reasoning about characters, motives, and outcomes. The advantage of this approach for a school is the ability to select readings that emphasize particular values. A school or school system could determine values to be taught in a literary program, then examine offerings from the Center for Learning to match target values and literary selections. Although much of the reading is at the high school level, there are ample selections cast at the elementary and middle school levels. This program could act as a basis of a values-based literature program or could be used to supplement materials already in use. Either way, these materials offer additional tools for the teacher or parent who is concerned about the role literature can play in character formation.

Getting Started

Any school concerned with the character of its students should seriously consider how literature can play a role in the development of good character. The following are suggestions on how to go about establishing or strengthening an existing program.

Teachers and parents can form a committee to meet and discuss readings that address the targeted values. A reading list should be compiled for each grade level so that students avoid reading the same book or short stories year after year. Readings should address significant issues but need to be appropriate for the students' reading level. In other words, Faulkner's *The Sound and the Fury* would not be appropriate for middle school and early high school students! The list must include narratives that reflect historical and philosophical perspectives. Excellent contemporary works should be included, but classic works should not be neglected.

Training should be provided for all teachers to insure that they have the skills to lead seminars or guided discussions with their students. Simply reading a wonderful text and having students answer questions at the end of the reading will not facilitate the development of character in students. The students must be engaged in the piece via discussions and writing opportunities. They must become participants in the piece, not passive recipients of information.

Finally, teacher and parent committees should revise and update the reading lists as they deem necessary. On the following pages is a grid taken from the Burlington City/Alamance County Schools in North Carolina. They adopted the Six Pillars of Character from the Josephson Institute of Ethics for their community focus. Each grade in the elementary schools and disciplines in the high schools correlated their readings to the character traits. Perhaps this grid could guide your efforts.

From the lap of a caring adult who reads aloud, children often develop a lifelong love of reading. The closeness and shared experience communicate to children that reading for pleasure is enjoyable and valued. As educators we should build on this experience, continuing it as long as possible. We may not hold many children in our laps, but we can hold them figuratively with our enthusiasm for reading and our choice of quality literature. When we encourage reading about great ideas of humanity, we open the door to the life of the mind. From this experience children transcend the immediate and engage in the possible. What a wonderful gift to give our children!

Grades K–1   REPRODUCIBLE WITH ATTRIBUTION TO BURLINGTON CITY/ALAMANCE COUNTY SCHOOLS, NORTH CAROLINA—CHARACTER READING LIST

Title	Trustworthiness	Respect	Responsibility	Fairness	Caring	Citizenship
MYSELF (BANNERS UNIT)						
Daniel's Dog	•		•			
The Snowy Day		•		•		
Chester's Way	•	•			•	
General Store		•			•	
Is This for You?		•	•		•	
HOLIDAYS (BANNERS UNIT)						
Lion Dancer	•	•				
Las Nandades		•				•
Valentine Friends						
Celebrations		•		•		•
It's Thanksgiving	•					•
The Halloween Performance		•				•
HOMES (BANNERS UNIT)						
Yonder	•		•		•	
Home in the Sky			•		•	
A Clean House for Mole & Mouse			•		•	
This Is the Place for Me		•			•	
How a House is Built				•		
The Big Orange Splot			•		•	•
A House Is a House for Me	•				•	
OTHER BOOKS (NOT BANNERS)						
The Foolish Tortoise					•	
The Greedy Python			•			•
Franklin Fibs						
What Mark Jo Shared				•	•	
Tyrone the Double Dirty Rotten Cheater						
Tyrone the Horrible			•		•	•

121

REPRODUCIBLE WITH ATTRIBUTION TO BURLINGTON CITY/ALAMANCE COUNTY SCHOOLS, NORTH CAROLINA—CHARACTER READING LIST

Grades 2 Title	Trustworthiness	Respect	Responsibility	Fairness	Caring	Citizenship
Horton Hatches the Egg	•					
George & Martha Stories	•					
Amelia Bedelia	•					
Amazing Grace	•					•
Ira Sleeps Over	•					
Charlie and the Chocolate Factory			•			
Mrs. Piggle Wiggle Books	•	•	•	•		•
Berenstein Bear Books	•	•				
Miss Nelson Books		•				
Leo the Late Bloomer		•			•	
Perfect the Pig		•				
Alexander's Terrible, Horrible, No Good,...			•			
Make Way for Ducklings			•		•	
Three Bears			•		•	
Best Friends			•	•	•	
Big Orange Splot				•		
Cinderella				•		
Rough Face Girl				•		
Freckles and Willie					•	
I'll Love You Forever					•	
I'll Always Love You					•	
Garden Gates						
Max						
Nate the Great	•	•				
Ugly Duckling		•				
Keep the Lights Burning, Abbie			•		•	•
The Story of Johnny Appleseed					•	
Daniel's Duck					•	
Train Set					•	

Grades 3   REPRODUCIBLE WITH ATTRIBUTION TO BURLINGTON CITY/ALAMANCE COUNTY SCHOOLS, NORTH CAROLINA—CHARACTER READING LIST

Title	Trustworthiness	Respect	Responsibility	Fairness	Caring	Citizenship
Charlotte's Web	•		•		•	•
Ramona Quimby, Age 3		•	•		•	•
Castles of Sand						
When I Was Nine			•		•	
Thy Friend Obadiah	•		•		•	•
Pilgrim Times			•			•
Granddaddy's Place	•					
The White Stallion			•			
Mr. Peaceable Paints		•			•	
Tim to the Rescue					•	
The Sea of Gold			•			
Monkey and the Crocodile	•			•		
The House on East 88th Street				•	•	
Jason						
Recital		•	•		•	
Phyliss Wheatty	•					
Alexander's Terrible, Horrible, No Good...		•	•	•		
Forecast						
Words In Our Hands				•	•	
The Horse who Lived Upstairs				•	•	•
Mufaro's Beautiful Daughter	•				•	
The Boy Who Cried Wolf	•					
Piglet Meets a Heffalump			•			

Grades 4

Title	Trustworthiness	Respect	Responsibility	Fairness	Caring	Citizenship
RESERVED NOVELS						
Tales of a Fourth-Grade Nothing					•	
Mr. Popper's Penguin			•		•	•
Stone Fox		•		•	•	
The Mouse and the Motorcycle						
How to Eat Fried Worms	•					
American Tall Tales	•				•	
Be a Perfect Person In Just Three Days			•			
Beezus and Ramona			•		•	
Caddie Woodlawn			•			
Charlotte's Web	•		•			
Chocolate Fever			•			
Class President	•	•	•	•		•
The Cricket in the Square						
Encyclopedia Brown Series			•			
The Enormous Egg			•			•
The Fantastic Mr. Fox			•			
The Giving Tree			•		•	
How to Fight a Girl						
The Hundred Dresses					•	
Hurray for Ali Baba Berenstein					•	
Jelly Belly					•	•
Little House on the Prairie	•		•			
Moss Gown					•	
Mighty Nightmare						
Phoebe the Spy	•				•	
Rabbit Hill	•		•		•	
The Reluctant Dragon						
Scared Silly					•	

Grades 5   REPRODUCIBLE WITH ATTRIBUTION TO BURLINGTON CITY/ALAMANCE COUNTY SCHOOLS, NORTH CAROLINA—CHARACTER READING LIST

Title	Trustworthiness	Respect	Responsibility	Fairness	Caring	Citizenship
RESERVED NOVELS						
Pinballs	•	•	•	•	•	•
Maniac Magee	•	•	•		•	
Dear Mrs. Henshaw			•	•		
Indian in the Cupboard			•			
A Taste of Blackberries					•	
A Christmas Carol						
Ben and Me			•			
Charlie and the Chocolate Factory	•		•	•		•
Homer Price	•					•
The Incredible Journey	•	•	•		•	
The Lion, the Witch, and the Wardrobe						
Make Four Million Dollars by Thursday		•	•	•		
Sadako and the Thousand Paper Cranes	•				•	•
Sarah, Plain and Tall	•					
The Secret Garden	•					
Trumpet of the Swans	•		•	•	•	•
Tuck Everlasting	•					
The War with Grandpa	•				•	
The Wish Giver			•	•		

Grades 6

Title	Trustworthiness	Respect	Responsibility	Fairness	Caring	Citizenship
The Black Pearl		•	•			
The Endless Steppe					•	•
Mixed-up Files of Mrs. Basil E. Frankweller	•	•		•		•
Monkey Island			•		•	
Number The Stars	•		•	•	•	•
The Secret Garden			•	•	•	•
Sounder	•		•	•	•	
Where the Red Fern Grows	•	•	•		•	•
The Witch of Blackbird Pond					•	
Zlata's Diary			•			
SHORT STORIES						
Becky and the Wheels and Brake Boys	•	•			•	•
Carrying the Running-	•					
Fire	•		•			
President Cleveland			•			•
The Scribe				•	•	•
Sweet Summer		•		•	•	•
Tuesday of the Other June				•		
The White Umbrella			•	•		
PLAYS						
A Christmas Carol		•			•	
Riddles in the Dark	•		•			
The Secret Garden	•	•	•		•	
A Shipment of Mute Fate				•		
You're a Good Man, Charlie Brown		•			•	•
POETRY						
Common Bond					•	
Foreign Student					•	•
Legacy			•			•

Grades 7

Title	Trustworthiness	Respect	Responsibility	Fairness	Caring	Citizenship
The Adventures of Tom Sawyer	•					•
Call of the Wild	•				•	
Anne Frank: Diary of a Young Girl		•	•	•	•	•
Dicey's Song			•	•	•	
The Good Earth		•	•	•	•	
Jonathan Livingston Seagull	•					
Kidnapped	•		•			•
The Pearl				•	•	
The Red Pony	•		•	•		
Roll of Thunder, Hear My Cry			•			•
A Solitary Blue			•			
SHORT STORIES						
All Summer in a Day	•	•		•		
Charles	•	•				
Gentlemen of Rio en Medio				•		
The Old Demon			•			•
The Ransom of Red Chief			•			
Rikki-tikki-tavi					•	
A Secret for Two					•	
Zoo					•	
PLAYS						
Scrooge & Marley: A Christmas Carol		•				•
Driving Miss Daisy	•	•				
Grandpa and the Statue	•		•		•	
The Monsters are Due on Maple Street	•				•	
POETRY						
The Courage that My Mother Had					•	
If I Can Stop One Heart From Breaking					•	
I'm Nobody		•				

127

Grade 8

Title	Trustworthiness	Respect	Responsibility	Fairness	Caring	Citizenship
The Chocolate War		•	•			
The Giver		•	•	•	•	
To Kill a Mockingbird	•		•	•	•	•
The Outsiders	•		•	•	•	
The Pigman	•		•	•	•	•
Ransom			•	•	•	•
The Red Badge of Courage					•	
The Scarlet Letter				•		•
The Weirdo			•		•	•
Where the Lilies Bloom			•		•	
SHORT STORIES						
The Adventure of the Speckled Bird	•	•		•		
Charles	•	•				
Christmas Day in the Morning	•			•	•	
The Finish of Patsy Barnes	•			•	•	
Flowers for Algernon	•			•	•	
A Retrieved Reformation				•		
Thank You, Ma'am				•	•	
PLAYS						
A Raisin in the Sun	•		•		•	
Romeo & Juliet/West Side Story	•					
POETRY						
Barbara Frichie	•	•	•		•	
For My Sister Who In The Fifties		•			•	
O Captain! My Captain!						
Paul Revere's Ride						
RECOMMENDED READING LIST						
Flowers for Algernon		•	•		•	
Freak the Mighty		•		•		

High School

REPRODUCIBLE WITH ATTRIBUTION TO BURLINGTON CITY/ALAMANCE COUNTY SCHOOLS, NORTH CAROLINA—CHARACTER READING LIST

Title	Trustworthiness	Respect	Responsibility	Fairness	Caring	Citizenship
NOVELS						
All Quiet on the Western Front	•	•	•			•
Animal Farm	•	•	•			•
Anthem	•	•	•			•
David Copperfield	•		•		•	
Anne Frank: Diary of a Young Girl	•		•		•	•
Frankenstein	•		•		•	
The Good Earth			•			
Lord of the Flies	•	•	•		•	
1984						
A Tale of Two Cities	•	•	•		•	
Things Fall Apart	•		•	•	•	•
VIDEOS						
Excaliber						
Gandhi	•					
Guns of August						
Oliver						
Rise and Fall of the Third Reich						
Schindler's List						
POETRY & EPICS						
The Aeneid						
Beowulf	•					
The Canterbury Tales						
Egyptian Poets (selections)						
England in 1819	•	•			•	
The Epic of Gilgamesh						
If						
Iliad	•					
Inferno	•					

High School   (Continued...)   REPRODUCIBLE WITH ATTRIBUTION TO BURLINGTON CITY/ALAMANCE COUNTY SCHOOLS, NORTH CAROLINA—CHARACTER READING LIST

Title	Trustworthiness	Respect	Responsibility	Fairness	Caring	Citizenship
POETRY CONT...						
Li Po, Selected Works		•	•			•
Odyssey	•	•	•			•
On His Blindness						
Paradise Lost						
Pilgrim's Progress	•	•	•			
The Rubaiyat						
Russia 1812						
The Seafarer						
Sir Gawain and the Green Knight		•				
Song of Roland	•	•	•			
The Thousand and One Nights						
Ulysses						
The Wanderer						
DRAMA						
Antigone (Jean Anouilh)	•	•	•	•	•	•
Antigone (Sophocles)	•	•	•	•	•	•
Cyrano de Bergerac		•				
A Doll's House						
Everyman						
Faust						
Hamlet						
Joan of Arc						
Julius Caesar						
Macbeth						
A Man for All Seasons						
Medea						
Merchant of Venice						
Oedipus						
Othello						

High School   (Continued...)   REPRODUCIBLE WITH ATTRIBUTION TO BURLINGTON CITY/ALAMANCE COUNTY SCHOOLS, NORTH CAROLINA—CHARACTER READING LIST

Title	Trustworthiness	Respect	Responsibility	Fairness	Caring	Citizenship
Pygmalion	•	•	•	•	•	•
Romeo & Juliet	•	•	•	•	•	•
Tartuffe			•			•
SHORT SELECTIONS						
Aesop's Fables	•	•	•			•
The African Child (excerpts)	•	•				
African Proverbs		•				
Analects		•				
The Apology (excerpts)	•	•			•	
Athenian Oath			•			
The Babur Nama (excerpts)			•			
The Beggar						
The Bible (excerpts: Parables, Prodigal Son, Good Samaritan, Story of Ruth, Job, Sermon on the Mount, Book of Psalms, Ten Commandments)		•	•	•		
Candide (excerpts)			•			•
A Child's Christmas in Wales						
Dead Men's Path						
Don Quixote (excerpts)	•	•			•	
Fairy Tales						
The False Gems						
Hammurabi's Code						
Here I Stand: Biography of Martin Luther	•		•			•
Hippocratic Oath						
History of the Peloponnesian War, Speech From Pericles' Funeral						•
How Much Land Does Man Need?						
Kaffir Boy (excerpts)	•	•		•	•	•
The Koran (excerpts)	•					
The Last Lesson			•			
Les Miserables (excerpts)	•		•	•	•	•

High School (Continued . . .)

REPRODUCIBLE WITH ATTRIBUTION TO BURLINGTON CITY/ALAMANCE COUNTY SCHOOLS, NORTH CAROLINA—CHARACTER READING LIST

Title	Trustworthiness	Respect	Responsibility	Fairness	Caring	Citizenship
Magna Carta						•
Masnavi	•					
The Metamorphosis	•					
Mythology	•					
No Witchcraft for Sale						
The Overcoat	•					
The Prince (excerpts)		•				
The Rat Trap						
The Republic (excerpts)	•					
The Rockinghorse Winner			•			
The Social Contract (excerpts)						
The Spirit of Laws (excerpts)						
Three Baskets of Wisdom						
Treasury of African Folklore (selections)						
Two Treatises on Government (excerpts)						
A Vindication of the Rights of Women						
WORLD LITERARY & HISTORICAL RESOURCES— NOVELS						
Black Boy	•	•	•	•	•	•
The Grapes of Wrath		•				
The Great Gatsby	•	•	•			
I Know Why the Caged Bird Sings						
Native Son	•	•		•		•
Of Mice and Men	•				•	
The Red Badge of Courage						•
The Scarlet Letter						
A Separate Peace						
To Kill a Mockingbird	•		•	•	•	

High School (Continued...)

Title	Trustworthiness	Respect	Responsibility	Fairness	Caring	Citizenship
DRAMA						
The Crucible	•	•	•	•	•	
Death of a Salesman	•	•	•	•	•	•
The Glass Menagerie					•	•
Grandpa and the Statue	•	•	•			•
The Miracle Worker		•				•
Our Town						
A Raisin in the Sun	•	•	•	•	•	•
VIDEOS						
Glory	•		•	•	•	•
Gideon's Trumpet	•	•	•	•	•	•
Eyes on the Prize				•		
Letters Home from Vietnam			•			
Apollo 13			•			
Roots				•		
All the President's Men						
Roll of Thunder, Hear My Cry						
POETRY						
In Honor of David Brooks, My Father		•				
Any Human to Another	•				•	
If You Were Coming in the Fall	•			•		•
Tell All the Truth						
Douglass	•					
The Haunted Oak						•
The Death of the Hired Man						
Mending Wall						•
Neither Out Far Nor in Deep						
I, Too	•		•	•	•	•
God's Trombones						
Evangeline	•			•	•	

High School (Continued...)

Title	Trustworthiness	Respect	Responsibility	Fairness	Caring	Citizenship
"Butch" Weldy			•			•
America				•		•
I Hear America Singing						•
SHORT SELECTIONS						
All Summer in a Day		•	•	•		•
Antaeus						
Blues Ain't No Mockingbird	•				•	
By Waters of Babylon	•	•		•	•	•
The Egg						
A Man Called Horse			•			
Maud Martha						
The Minister's Black Veil	•			•		
My Oedipus Complex		•				
An Occurrence at Owl Creek Bridge	•					
The Open Boat			•		•	
Poison						
Rules of the Game				•		•
The Scarlet Ibis		•			•	
The Sniper						
Thank you, Ma'am					•	
The Women from Brewster Place	•	•		•		
NON-FICTION						
Aphorisms			•			•
The Autobiography (excerpts)	•			•		•
Boy Scout Oath						
A Christmas Memory					•	
Civil Disobedience (excerpts)						
Common Sense, No. 1						
The Declaration of Independence	•					
Gettysburg Address						•

High School   (Continued...)   REPRODUCIBLE WITH ATTRIBUTION TO BURLINGTON CITY/ALAMANCE COUNTY SCHOOLS, NORTH CAROLINA — CHARACTER READING LIST

Title	Trustworthiness	Respect	Responsibility	Fairness	Caring	Citizenship
Girl Scout Promise	•	•	•	•	•	•
I Have a Dream	•	•	•	•	•	•
Kennedy's Inaugural Address	•	•	•			•
My Bondage and My Freedom (excerpts)	•	•	•			•
A Narrative of Her Captivity			•			•
Nature (excerpts)	•		•			
Of Plymouth Plantation			•			•
Roots (excerpts)	•		•			
Sayings of Poor Richard			•			
Self-Reliance	•		•			
Sinners in the Hands of an Angry God						
Speech to the Virginia Convention	•			•		•
Up From Slavery (excerpts)	•		•	•		•
Walden (excerpts)						

Chapter 7

Service Learning

At Winona Senior High School in Winona, Minnesota, service learning is an essential part of the school curriculum. Senior students serve for 90 minutes a day, four days a week, at service placements ranging from early childhood special education to hospice care. A large number of students choose to assist in elementary classrooms. Other sites include Head Start, English as a second language classes, preschool and day-care settings, and agencies serving the severely mentally and emotionally impaired. A fifth day of the week is set aside for class discussions and workshops on topics such as effective techniques to deal with Alzheimer's patients. Students are required to do formal research papers and keep a daily reflective journal. Other, shorter assignments require analytic skills. (Institute for Global Ethics, 1996, p. 16)

In Tacoma, Washington, a hospital physical therapist sent a videotape of an 18-month-old child with multiple sclerosis to a high school industrial design class. The students in the class designed and built a wheelchair that had the capacity to be enlarged as the child grew. Students applied technical knowledge and problem-solving skills to this project and were rewarded with a feeling of great joy as they saw the smiles of gratitude from the child and his parents. (Kinsley and McPherson, 1995, p. 87)

At a South Central Los Angeles high school, students raise and market "Food From the 'Hood" (including a natural foods salad dressing called "Straight Out the Garden") to raise money to rebuild their community and fund college scholarships. On an Evergreen, Washington, middle school campus, an entire student body voted to build and operate the area's first native plant wetland nursery to restore local stream beds. In rural Minnesota, a third grade class, in order to renovate their city's neglected rest stop on the state highway, prepared a plan, secured governmental approval, raised resources, and completed the painting and landscaping required to give the place new life. (Kinsley and McPherson, p. 101)

Look at what all of these examples have in common. Each has students committing to helping others—giving of their time to assist others. Should this be surprising? A survey by Independent Sector, a nonprofit organization that promotes giving, found that 61% of youths 12-17 years old volunteered about three hours a week, and that teens were four times as likely to volunteer when asked than when they were not. Of those who were asked to volunteer, 90% did. Bruce Bolton, in a report titled "Their Best Selves: Building Character Education and Service Learning Together in the Lives of Young People," cites a 1996 survey done by UCLA's Higher Education Research Institute that found that 71.8 % of those polled had done some volunteer work in the past year, compared to 62% in 1989. Some 38.4% were spending an hour a week as volunteers, compared to 26.6% in 1987—a 31% gain. (p. 10)

This doesn't surprise me. In my travels around the country, I continually find students and teachers working together in service projects ranging from food drives to assisting individuals seriously impacted by natural or personal disasters. When I ask them about their service experiences, nearly all students respond that they are/were positive experiences. Some cited personal or moral growth as an outcome. Others said that serving others is practicing what the Bible demands. Still others described how they felt better about themselves after serving others. All of these responses have been shown to be attributed to service learning. D. Conrad and D. Hedin, in a report titled "High School Community Service: A Review of Research and Programs" (1989), noted that service learning helps promote:

- Self-esteem
- Personal efficacy (sense of worth and competence)
- Ego and moral development
- Exploration of new roles, identities and interests
- Willingness to take risks, accept new challenges
- Revised and reinforced values and beliefs
- Taking responsibility for, accepting consequences of own actions (cited in Kinsley and McPherson, p. 5)

Recall any time you volunteered to assist others. Perhaps you're a Scout leader, or Sunday School teacher, or book-fair manager at your elementary school. Perhaps your church group or service club built a wheelchair ramp at someone's home. Perhaps you teach reading to adults or serve dinner at the homeless shelter. Perhaps you merely went to shovel snow from an elderly neighbor's walk, or you used your own trash bag to pick up around the Little League bleachers. Maybe you went with a group of teenagers to help clean a stream or rebuild an elderly person's storm-damaged home. In every case, you easily could have filled the time with other activities with your family. It probably took up weekend time you might have spent recharging your own batteries. You may have momentarily resented the commitment you made as you left for a pledged involvement. But what small miracle happens to your attitude once you start doing the work? You realize it's you who's benefiting the most from donating your time and energy. You feel spiritually enlarged, connected and involved in a wider community. An old maxim describes it: "The more you give the more you receive." When our students engage in service learning, they, too, learn the meaning of this maxim.

We change for the better when we serve others. Each of us benefits from the serving experience more than the person being served. Somehow a recipient's gratitude feels better and lasts longer than someone's words of praise. If you're ever feeling low about yourself or your circumstances, you can always find relief in helping someone else. Serving others unites the mind and heart, and connects the individual to the larger community of man.

Service learning is essential to developing empathy and responsiveness, important traits of good character. Any school that hopes to be successful in a character education initiative needs to establish service learning as a critical element of their efforts. Bruce Bolton, in "Their Best Selves," illustrates a "Four-Way Fit" between service and character education.

- First, service learning renders concrete the abstractions of moral teaching.
- Second, the emotional satisfaction students gain from being involved in service to others and from a job well done, imparts feeling of self-worth that reverberates beyond individual lives.

- Third, the structure of service learning activities fosters the development of such values as self-discipline and fidelity to a commitment.
- Fourth, and perhaps the most important, the experience of many service learning teachers and programs is that providing young people with opportunities to serve changes them and moves them in a positive direction: quite simply, it builds character. (pp. 10-11)

Elaborating a little more on Bolton's wonderful outline, it is critically important that students apply the concrete to the abstract. It does little good to read about people's needs or to hear words of kindness unless these are applied. Mother Teresa's unstinting works of compassion may seem to be more service than we want to commit to, but any child or student who demonstrates kindness in the school or community is feeling some of the same joy and calling that Mother Teresa knew.

Several years ago a high school student who was working with elementary children noted, for the first time, how poor some of the children were, and his view toward these children changed. He had read about poverty and had talked in classes and with peers about poverty, but now he could see it manifested every day. The important lesson he learned is that physical poverty does not translate to poverty of the mind or heart. Because of his service learning, the education of his mind was being altered by the experiences of his heart.

When students commit to serving others, they come to learn that someone is counting on them. Though they might easily ignore taking out the trash at home, it's harder for them to ignore responsibilities to people outside the family who depend on them. The obligation helps them forge that mental connection that their word means something. They are expected to follow through because others count on them. What a great lesson to learn and carry through life—that my wants and needs must be weighed with the wants and needs of others.

Service learning often seems to generate self-respect for a job well done even more than a paying job. Both the heart and mind are committed to the effort to create a positive outcome. The feeling of emotional satisfaction is so rewarding for many students that they incorporate community service in the rest of their lives. A student who serves learns in the best way possible to "know, love, and do the good."

A good service learning program for children will not come easily. I believe that a school should first examine its own culture. Is the school as a whole a caring place? Do the adults model caring towards the students? To develop an "ethos" of caring in a school, all individuals who come in contact with children must model caring and kindness. This begins with a kind crossing guard, bus drivers who know their children's names, a custodian who enjoys showing children how to do things. It's demonstrated by teachers who speak respectfully to students and go the extra mile to assist students. It's supported by expectations of a safe and orderly learning climate.

Teaching children to care is not something that can be done through explanation or command. It must be modeled by adults in school. Students mimic what they see. If teachers or staff shout at students, publicly embarrass wrongdoers, or put down students with sarcasm in class, the school does not offer a caring, nurturing environment, and the art of caring will not develop among children. Those who develop these traits will do so only if they have outside influences to encourage a civic attitude. The school is missing a wonderful opportunity to make the community better for itself.

In considering a service learning program, we should not underestimate the power and ability of our students to reach out to others. I have witnessed many wonderful acts of unexpected kindness toward students and others done by my own students. Several times I revised my attitude toward a child after noting a particular act of service toward another. The Cuban revolution offers us an example of what youth are capable of doing. Jonathan Kozol's *Children of the Revolution* (1978) tells the story of how 100,000 Cuban youths, 10-19 years old, volunteered to live in the country to help with the literacy program among the peasants. In one year's time, functional illiteracy was virtually eliminated. It is not important what we think about the Cuban revolution, but that we recognize what the Cuban students were capable of doing.

To be successful, we must organize. Service both within and outside the school will demand a certain structure to help insure its continuation and success. Some more mature students will be able to formulate and determine their projects of serving both inside and outside the school arena. Remember that age is not the determining factor. Children who have matured in homes and schools where service is valued will have experiences that may foster independence of thought and action. Other students may need more structure and clear guidance for creating an awareness, asking for help, arranging the time for the service, and monitoring. This calls for greater commitment from the supervisor, whether an adult or another student.

Service can occur both inside and outside the school environment. First let's examine service learning within the schools.

Service Learning Within the School

We don't need to reinvent the wheel on how to create caring opportunities for students. Many schools and school systems create an environment of caring through service toward others and have programs in place. While working in Ft. Walton Beach, Florida, I saw a wonderful example of service learning. The fourth graders assisted the arriving kindergartners learn to go through the cafeteria line, choose their food and drinks, sit down and eat appropriately. This "mentoring" was supposed to last two to three weeks, but at the end of the second week, all the fourth graders asked for a meeting with the principal. They declared that they wanted to continue to eat with their "K" buddies. They claimed if they weren't there to have lunch with the kindergartners, the five-year-olds wouldn't know what to do—their buddies needed them. I later learned that the fourth graders were forfeiting some of their recess to eat lunch with the kindergartners, yet they wanted to continue the arrangement. Might they have been benefiting as much as the kindergartners?

Character educator Thomas Lickona, in *Educating for Character* (1991), cites several examples of how schools can nurture a caring environment through service within the school. The Walt Disney Elementary School in San Ramon, California, has a system called Class Buddies, whereby older students work with younger students. Fifth graders may work with third graders, and third graders read to kindergarten students. In Ontario, Canada, kindergarten students at the Emily Carr School are placed with 9- to 12-year-old students who have learning disabilities. The kindergarten teacher, Dee Brent, describes the change in the learning-disabled students:

> It makes them feel so valuable. Their reading scores have shot up; they've spent a lot of time looking for books to read to the little ones. In the fall they organized a science treasure hunt for their little buddies. There is

real affection; the older kids will poke their heads in to say "hi" when they go by, and my children will say to me, "I saw my buddy on Saturday!" The experience has been especially important for one older boy who has virtually no support at home. Here he has three little ones who love him. (p. 314)

John Arnold, in his book *Visions of Teaching and Learning* (1990), cites the Helping Hands program of Jefferson Middle School in Champaign, Illinois, as an example of a school-oriented service program. The program, established in 1978, offers seventh and eighth grade students an opportunity to engage in peer-helping experiences. Some examples of their opportunities are:

Pal Program—Seventh and eighth grade students "pal up" with a sixth grader who may need an extra friend.

Tutoring Groups—After-school tutoring, either individually or in small groups, is provided for students needing additional help.

TMH Class—Reading and just socializing with trainable mentally handicapped students.

Deborah Kasak, a counselor at the school, recognizes that students gain much from the experience. She is quoted in Arnold's book:

Students develop a strong sense of responsibility and commitment to their group projects and feel pride when they contribute to someone else's happiness. (p. 143)

Cynthia Parsons, in her fine book, *Service Learning From A–Z* (1991), offers numerous suggestions on service opportunities for students in the school.

1. For every non-English-speaking preschooler, prepare alphabet and number books in English and the preschooler's own language; have the books focus on community service centers and significant buildings. (p. 6)

2. Have every civics class sponsor and tutor at least one immigrant each term. Imagine the kindness the children would show to someone struggling to understand the principles of democratic government and its special form in the United States. (This could be offered during school and/or immediately after school.) (p. 58)

3. Middle school students (10- to 14-year-olds) might run after-school recreation programs for 5- to 9-year-olds who otherwise would be "latch-key" children (assuming the school grounds are the same). (p. 88)

Teaching Caring via Service Outside the School

Although schools can offer wonderful opportunities for the practice of caring behavior through service to other students, many additional opportunities exist outside the school environment. Schools need to network with service agencies and religious organizations to determine community needs and how their students might fit in. An example might be an agency's service project to help winterize houses of the poor and elderly. Students could volunteer to assist in this project on Saturdays. Another program could be to have students help staff soup kitchens during the weekend or even during the week if logistics regarding transportation, school schedules, etc., could be arranged.

John Arnold (1993) notes that community service projects offer powerful learning opportunities for adolescents. He cites as an example Challenger Middle School in Colorado Springs, Colorado. Every team (middle schools are often divided into teams) has its students involved in service projects through its H.U.G.S.S. (Helping Us Grow through Service and Smiles) program. At Shoreham-Wading River Middle School in Shoreham, New York, all students participate in service projects that are integrated into the curriculum. For example, students may work in nursing homes while they are studying the aging process. Arnold (1990) also recognizes the "Whobodies" of Bryan Junior High School in Elmhurst, Illinois. To belong to the Whobodies, one only needs to practice care and love. As it turns out, Whobodies comprises two-thirds of the student body. Some of their projects are:

- The adoption of animals of the Brookfield Zoo
- Visiting patients at local hospitals
- Distribution of leaflets concerning a stress-management workshop after a local disaster
- Collecting toys for the Marine Corps' Toys for Tots campaign
- Organizing a program for Down Syndrome students

Service learning has become a focus in the middle schools of Hickory, North Carolina. The service learning plan, Students Engaged in Responsible Visionary Endeavors (SERVE), introduces service learning in the sixth grade with an emphasis on service to self and team. The developmental approach to introducing service learning into the school curriculum has worked very well for College Park Middle School in Hickory. SERVE was developed to "provide students with opportunities for service to others in school and in the community and fill the critical need to help students build self-esteem and learn the skills necessary to become responsible citizens at school and home and in the community." What is interesting in the developmental approach from sixth to eighth grade. The sixth grade focus is on "Service to Self and Team"; the seventh grade focus is on "Service to School"; and the eighth grade focus is on "Service to Community."

In the sixth grade, students learn about the obligations they have toward each other. This includes encouragement of others as well as the avoidance of "put-downs." In advisor-advisee (for those not familiar with middle schools, think of this as a nurturing, supportive homeroom time), they explore causes of conflict from both global and local perspectives. One activity was making 1,000 origami paper cranes, which were sent to the Children's Peace Monument in Hiroshima, Japan. The advisor-advisee groups also do monthly collections for the Salvation Army soup kitchen and spend one hour a week reading to kindergarten students at a nearby elementary school. Sixth grade teams worked on a fundraiser for a school in Missouri needing help after the 1993 floods.

The seventh grade focus extends beyond a team or advisor/advisee group and involves service to the entire school. Among the activities are a weekly closed-circuit television broadcast, an active pep club to encourage school spirit, development of a pamphlet for new students about the school and community, an environmental focus for school cleanup and beautification, and a special decorated dining area in the cafeteria for students at each grade level who are recognized and selected by their teammates as "Citizens of the Week." These individuals can bring a friend to lunch. In addition, there are strong efforts to raise funds for the homeless and hungry people in the geographical area.

Finally in the eighth grade, the strategy is to have students serve the community beyond the school. All eighth graders are challenged to perform 10 hours of community service. Each team has adopted a service agency, and the students do a variety of activities based on the needs of the agencies. Their projects have included assisting in the community soup kitchen and Salvation Army shelter, and sponsoring a monthly birthday party for adults at an adult day care center. During advisor-advisee time, the teachers and students reflect on the service learning experiences. Each volunteer also keeps a journal as part of the evaluation procedure. The journals must describe not only the activities, but also the student's personal reactions to the internship.

Maintaining a journal is important if students are to learn and grow from the service experience. Norman Sprinthall (1994) notes that "so-called 'service learning' or various kinds of volunteer work may not have any noticeable developmental impact [the ability to reflect on the significance of the experience both as a means to develop positive ego development and moral thinking] without guided reflection." His research indicates that if students can reflect on their experiences, using a seminar/discussion session and journal writings, they are able to develop greater ethical insights into their efforts. This is critically important for all service learning, whether in or outside of the school. Time should be allowed for students to talk about their experiences, write in journals, and receive feedback regarding their insights with the intention of helping the interns develop greater insight into the experiences. James and Pamela Toole, co-directors of the Compass Institute and National Youth Leadership Council of St. Paul, Minnesota, have developed a Service Learning Cycle. Notice how the cycle places great importance on constant reflection and growth of the server.

Middle schools are not the only ones offering wonderful service activities for students. Chattanooga School of the Arts and Sciences, a K-12 school, has an active service component. One especially wonderful project is the school's link with the Chattanooga Home for Seniors. At some time during the school year, all 1,100 students participate in work there, either painting rooms and doing yardwork, or entertaining residents and taking oral histories.

High schools throughout America are also actively involved in service learning. Gig Harbor High School in Gig Harbor, Washington, is but one example. It has service as an integral part of the total high school curriculum, and the students have done a variety of projects. The Spanish classes wrote and translated children's stories into Spanish, and the drawing class illustrated them. These books were donated to the Martin Luther King, Jr. Shelter for homeless families to encourage

James and Pamela Toole,
Compass Institute and National Youth Leadership Council, 1991.
Revised 1993

Hispanic parents to read to their children. Gig Harbor students recently received a national award for their work with homeless children. The biology and ecology classes run a science lab at the neighboring elementary school five days a week. Members of the football team watch Monday night football with senior citizens at convalescent centers. Leadership students are mentors for at-risk elementary school children. Business education students serve as bookkeepers for FISH, the local food bank. (Kinsley and McPherson, p. 53) What a variety of experiences within Gig Harbor High School! Not only are these students developing compassion and generosity, and learning to live outside themselves, they're also bolstering their scholarship applications and beginner's resumes!

There are opportunities for anyone to find a place to serve others. Consider the following possibilities for service for your school:

WORK WITH HABITAT FOR HUMANITY. Many communities now have Habitat for Humanity organizations, which are constantly seeking volunteers to help individuals who, with their sweat equity, build a home.

WORK IN LOCAL HOSPITALS. Hospitals can always find use for good volunteers. These individuals can deliver flowers and mail, work as assistants to nurses, or play games with children who are in the hospital.

ORGANIZE CLEAN-UPS OF PARKS AND OTHER COMMUNITY PROPERTIES. In inner cities, volunteers have cleaned trash-strewn land to create recreational areas for neighborhood youngsters.

ADOPT A HIGHWAY. In North Carolina, citizens or groups can "adopt" a section of a highway and pick up litter at intervals to keep it clean.

VISIT SENIOR-CITIZEN HOMES. This is a wonderful time for many of our youth to get to know our senior citizens. An especially valuable project would be to create a mini-"Foxfire" and chronicle the histories of these people. As each senior citizen dies without sharing his or her life, an important historical resource dies.

In essence, all we need to do is examine the needs of our community and we will find ample, perhaps too many, people and organizations that need the help of our youth and ourselves.

Getting Started: School Service

The first question a school staff must ask itself is, "Is this a school where we are truly caring toward our students?" In other words, does the staff welcome the students daily and outwardly show that they care about them? The students will not adopt a caring attitude toward others unless they feel they themselves are cared about. To answer this, teachers and administrators must assess their school climate, perhaps through a survey of students, parents, and the community. If students perceive the school climate as not caring, or the school has some teachers who practice caring while others do not, in-service training programs will be needed to help all teachers understand why a caring environment is crucial to developing students who care.

Assuming that the staff does cares about its students, and demonstrates it, you must then decide how to develop in students caring behavior toward others through service. The staff, students, and parents should develop a list of what constitutes caring behavior in the classroom. This can be done through a classroom meeting or through student government representatives. Ask students to brainstorm ways that they could help others. Then with this student input—perhaps coupled with ideas from parents and the community—develop a list of projects and activities. This could be shared with all students within the individual classroom or developed as a school-wide list of service opportunities. The staff should also identify opportunities in the school for students to be of service to others. They then choose which ones they want to do, according to their interests. Perhaps they "pal" with younger students, keep the school environment clean, help special needs students as the special needs children help others. The opportunities are limited only by your and your students' vision.

Those who practice service toward others, who act in a caring way at school, should be recognized publicly at school. Recognition can occur during announcements, bulletins, letters home to parents, or perhaps with bumper stickers that might say, "My Child Practices Service Toward Others at _____ School." I imagine many parents would love to display such a bumper sticker on their automobiles.

Service Projects Outside of School

The school should also determine opportunities for service outside the school. This will require working with community agencies and religious organizations, with special attention to transportation and other logistics. Make your efforts public. Invite the media to cover your projects. The more publicity you get, the more businesses and other organizations you'll find that are willing to support you and that will present opportunities. Contact all social service agencies for recommendations of individuals or groups that might appreciate volunteer help. Contact church groups, which may have ongoing projects that could use some kid power. Some sponsor trips to impoverished areas to assist needy residents.

Again, the students should be recognized for their work. Perhaps the agencies could take responsibility for providing this recognition. Newspapers should be encouraged to highlight student service volunteers. The key is to make the volunteerism meaningful to the students so that the importance of caring and service becomes a part of their character. There is an old African saying that it takes a village to raise a child. Service learning will demand the village. Can we call upon our village to help develop caring youth?

Chapter 8

Moving to Implementation

In the preceding chapters, I have presented five important aspects for schools to consider when establishing a program that seeks to develop character in students. Each of these practices, on its own, enhances a child's education by adding character development to academics. Together they offer a complete, integrated package of character education. Keep in mind that no character education program will be successful unless the adults—parents, teachers, school staff—model the traits we wish to develop in our students. These five areas are summarized below:

1. ESTABLISHMENT OF RULES AND PROCEDURES. Rules and procedures promote a business-like, productive, civil environment. With them in place, students know what is expected of them and how to go about their work. In addition, when students know and understand the school's rules and procedures, an environment is established where actions demonstrating character traits are practiced until they become habitual.

2. COOPERATIVE LEARNING. Students who work together during the normal academic class day recognize peers as having something worthy to contribute. It is easier to accomplish tasks when a group learns how to work together. Far too often teachers have students working by themselves, sitting in rows, forbidden to interact. Yet this is not how the real world operates. By working together we touch others and thereby become connected with some aspect of their lives.

3. TEACHING FOR THINKING. By incorporating the insights of Plato into our character development efforts, we recognize that thinking and reasoning skills are important in the development of character. The thinking skills students learn should be developmentally appropriate, with each skill building on previously learned ones and applied in the regular classroom curriculum. Students can apply these skills using a wide variety of academic methods and strategies, including thinking maps. Students, as they move towards the high school years, should make use of some ethical dilemmas, but this should not be their teachers' sole application of teaching for thinking.

4. READING FOR CHARACTER. Exposure to great literature and narratives brings students the joy that reading can provide. We should be careful to insure that our students are reading material that is worth reading and that provides strong examples of good character. Literature that is moving and offers ideas worth discussing is generally attractive to students. We should provide them reading that is also intellectually challenging and rich in opportunities for discussion of character. Selections should be taken from the best literature from throughout the world.

5. SERVICE LEARNING, BOTH WITHIN AND OUTSIDE THE SCHOOL ENVIRONMENT. Students should be given the opportunity to practice caring. For many students this is the beginning of assuming adult-like responsibilities and connecting with the world around them. Students who are involved in service learning develop the responsibility of helping provide for others' well being. Even in neighborhoods that are unsafe outside the school grounds, students can practice service within the safety of their school building. Service outside the school, and perhaps outside an immediate community, can be encouraged for all students. I feel this is especially critical for high school students as they are beginning to take their place as adults in our world.

For most schools, there is not enough time in the school day to add another program, even one as important as character education. But character education of the sort I advocate is *not* another "add-on" program. Most of work is done within the usual instructional day and within the curriculum. The service component may be an exception, but much of it can be planned within school hours. For some schools, the great majority of the service to others is done within the school curriculum. Character education asks us to rethink how we are teaching students and to include in our curriculum these five components of character development. Many of these curricular approaches are already in place in various schools. Our task is to make all of them an integrated part of our children's education.

Implementation

If we agree that character development has a role to play in the education of our students, our schools must begin developing the procedures that will insure our students develop good character. This may be the most difficult part of the plan. Many parents are justifiably concerned that proposed programs in character development will somehow resort to the now-discredited values-clarification-type programs. However, if school leaders show parents they are interested in the character development of their children, if they involve families in the decision making, and if they offer experiences that will meet these goals, support from parents and other community groups will generally be forthcoming.

Henry Huffman (1993), describes how his district, Mt. Lebanon School District in Pittsburgh, Pennsylvania, is working to implement a program on character education. After bringing in Thomas Lickona to talk to teachers and parents, district leaders developed a plan to include everyone in helping educate for character. I provide below their excellent outline in capital letters, offering my comments beside each step to assist those considering the adoption of a character education program such as I have proposed.

1. IDENTIFY A CORE OF DESIRED VIRTUES AS THE HEART OF CHARACTER EDUCATION EFFORTS. What are the values we wish to teach? The group is to determine the traits that promote civility and ethical strength that are to be intentionally taught to the children and modeled by the adults in the community. Input should be provided by teachers, parents, students, and other interested community members with a task force. Efforts must be made to create a bipartisan group of people to determine what values should be emphasized. Judith Hoffman and Anne R. Lee, in

Character Education Workbook for School Boards, Administrators & Community Leaders (1997) offer some solid ground rules for those wishing to create such a group:

We are all equal. Rules of civility begin with us.

- Task force members will be expected to work for consensus, resulting in a product that will have the support of the community.
- Each member will have an opportunity to speak on every issue but not monopolize the discussion.
- Task force members should feel free to express their convictions and concerns but always with a spirit of congeniality and respect.
- All points of view will be listened to respectfully.
- If the meeting becomes unproductive for any person, he or she should express this concern to the group.
- Task force meetings will be open to the public.
- The chairperson is the spokesperson for the task force. Any major concerns should be shared directly with the task force chairperson (p. 19-20).

2. PRESENT THE STRATEGIES TO THE STAFF AND THE COMMUNITY. This will entail a description of the goals of a character education program, which should be made available to members of the community. There are many ways to share the vision—by mailings or sent home from the school via the children. Television, radio, and the newspaper offer wonderful outlets to share the vision. Talks to the Chamber of Commerce, Rotary, Civitan and other like-minded groups can be crucial to building support. According to Edward DeRoche and Mary Williams in their book, *Educating Hearts and Minds: A Comprehensive Character Education Framework* (1998), gaining community consensus precedes successful implementation of a character education program in the schools. They propose that character education

- should reflect a concerted effort by the community and the schools (through its mission and goals) to educate children and youth about an agreed-on set of values.
- begins in a family setting.

- occurs when children and youth witness and imitate adults and peers modeling the consensus values.
- continues in the community (churches, youth groups, etc.) and in the schools.
- occurs when children and youth come to know the values through the school environment and its curriculum and co-curricular programs.
- occurs when children and youth have opportunities to study, clarify, reflect, reason, decide, and act on the values.
- is enhanced when children and youth are provided guided and supervised opportunities to engage in and practice the values.
- is verified or modified when participants assess the extent to which the programs and activities have met their mission, goals, and expectations.
- is verified when students and adults demonstrate and model the values.

Part or all of the above can be incorporated into your communication with the community. I would also recommend explaining to the community how practices such as the development of rules and procedures, cooperative learning, teaching for thinking, quality literature and narratives, and service learning will be used. This process helps a community understand that the interests of the school and the community are in touch. It also helps parents know that school administrators and teachers have carefully and thoroughly thought about the plan.

3. WRITE THE CORE VALUES INTO EXISTING K-12 CURRICULUM.
Assure teachers and parents that character development efforts will be based within the school curriculum. The strategies will change, but not the general curriculum. Teachers and parents should also know that character education will not be another "add-on" program. With all that is being asked of educators today, there is little or no time to place an add-on program in the curriculum. Our character-building efforts must reflect the ethos, or life, of the school. In the present proposal, the only program outside the traditional curriculum would be the service component (and in many schools, this is part of the curriculum). I believe this will not be a problem for parents who want their children to learn to take up responsibilities in the community and in the school.

4. ASK EACH SCHOOL IN THE DISTRICT TO WRITE A BEHAVIORAL CODE THAT REFLECTS THE CORE VALUES. Each school must develop ownership in its character development project. If the program is developed by the central office, the central office has the ownership, not the school, which must provide the services. Parents, teachers, and students should work together to develop a behavior code and mission statement that reflects the core values. This code should reflect the vision of what we want to be (i.e., what it looks and sounds like to be respectful, responsible, caring), as well as possible consequences for those who refuse to engage in civil behavior. Reflecting the goals of the school, the mission statement organizes the plan, which everyone is responsible for implementing.

5. ENCOURAGE ALL EMPLOYEE GROUPS TO ACKNOWLEDGE THEIR ROLE IN THE DEVELOPMENT OF ETHICAL STUDENTS. Bill Rauhauser, an old friend and one of the leading experts in the effective schools movement, told me that you can assess the climate of a school by talking to the janitor and the school secretary. To that I add lunchroom personnel as key climate indicators. Everyone in the school has a role to play in helping develop the character of the students. If it's left only to classroom teachers, important resources that exist throughout the school will be lost. The process of inclusion reinforces the valuable role that everyone in a school plays in the development of character.

6. PROVIDE AN ONGOING CHARACTER EDUCATION PARENTING PROGRAM FOR THE COMMUNITY. Schools play only part of the role needed to develop children of character. Family life is even more important. Give parents opportunities to attend training sessions on how to develop good character in their children at home. The district can offer overview programs on character education, and the schools can provide additional programs based on the particular needs of their students and parents. (Programs for parents of elementary school students may need to be different from programs for parents of middle or high school students.) Churches, synagogues, and temples, as well as other community organizations, can offer their expertise in helping mold the character of children. Schools must not depend solely

on their own staff to provide training or resources. Organizations such as "Cities in Schools" can also be helpful. Finally, PTAs (or PTOs) can create resource libraries for parents. Since they are often involved in fundraising activities, perhaps some books on parenting for character could be used as fundraisers. Helen LeGette's *Parents, Kids & Character: 21 Strategies to Help Your Children Develop Good Character* (1999) and Hal Urban's *Life's Greatest Lessons: 20 Things I Want My Kids to Know* (1997) are two books worthy of consideration.

7. DEVELOP COMMUNITY-SERVICE PROGRAMS AT BOTH ELEMENTARY AND SECONDARY LEVELS. We've discussed the importance of community service in character education programs. We must ask our community to help us provide opportunities for our students to become involved. One alternative school in Danville, Virginia, decided that all its students would begin each day doing 90 minutes of community service. The principal approached a rest home, an elementary school, and other nearby service providers. All agreed to have the students serve their clients, which they did by reading to youngsters and the elderly, and many other activities. The response was wonderful from the community and the students. But none of this would have happened unless the principal had asked the community for opportunities for his children to serve others. Remember, seek and ye shall find!

8. ASK EACH SCHOOL TO CREATE A CARING ENVIRONMENT THAT INSURES THE SUCCESS OF EACH STUDENT. Students don't care how much you know until they know how much you care! If school personnel do not manifestly care about students, no plan will help develop character in students. If students see teachers losing control, the message the teacher sends on "good days" will be greatly tempered by the reality the children see on "bad days." Once a school staff identifies the characteristics of a caring environment, it must develop procedures to insure that these characteristics are being modeled and taught on a daily basis.

These eight considerations call for the combined involvement of schools, homes, and communities in developing the character of children and students. This is a crucial lesson for those wishing to establish an educational program for character development. In developing the plan, we must seek to involve those who will be asked to help implement the plan. To do so will enable us to tap into the expertise and sensibility of the community in which we live. Remember, inclusion generally helps build responsibility and commitment.

In his fine article, "In Search of Effective Character Education" (1993), James Leming summarizes data on what we now know about programs oriented to character education. He concludes:

> Didactic methods alone—codes, pledges, teacher exhortation, and the like—are unlikely to have any significant or lasting effect on character.

> The development of students' capacity to reason about questions of moral conduct does not result in a related change in conduct. One cannot reason one's way to virtuous conduct. Character develops within a social web or environment. The nature of that environment, the messages it sends to individuals, and the behaviors it encourages and discourages are important factors to consider in character education. Clear rules of conduct, student ownership of those rules, a supportive environment, and satisfaction resulting from complying with the norms of the environment shape behavior.

> Character educators should not expect character formation to be easy or immediate. Nor should they expect prompt adoption of procedures leading to good habits. Those who expect easily achieved and dramatic effects will be disappointed. How many times do you have to remind your own children?

> Finally, those interested in character education have long believed that morally inspiring literature should be a part of any character education program. Surprisingly, not one research study has attempted to assess whether reading such literature has the expected effect on character. (p. 69)

To reiterate my perspective on character education: If you want to make permanent changes in the attitudes and beliefs of children as they grow to adulthood, you must model good behavior and right conduct and explain to the children what good practices you expect of them. Repeating slogans like "Just say no!" or "Resist the urgin'...stay a virgin!" will have no deep impact or lasting effect on a person's character. The same applies to giving a wonderful lecture or sermon.

Everyone may feel inspired at the time, buoyed by the speaker's enthusiasm, but after several days the effect disappears unless it is coupled with supporting strategies or practices.

I believe the goal of developing the character of our students is attainable by all schools. The development of character will demand that we, as educators, parents, and community leaders, get together and plan a program that will benefit our children, community and, ultimately, our nation. We can no longer wait for someone else to light our path. We know enough to begin the process. The question is whether we have the will to do so. I am sensing we have this will. More and more individuals are concerned about our youth and the character traits they'll need to become successful in both their communities and their careers.

I hope you agree with the approach I advance. But even if you don't, I applaud your concern about this important issue. I believe that the populace can no longer wait until some other "new" idea comes along, or until another idea emerges from academia. We don't need a new idea. Character education, combined with academic competency, represents the oldest mission of schools. Let's just focus on what we know in our hearts is true: that developing a child's journey of a thousand miles begins with the first step. Perhaps it's time for someone in your school or community to begin this walk so others may follow. If we believe in the future of our children, we must take this critically important step.

References

Introduction

Himmelfarb, Gertrude. *The De-moralization of Society: From Victorian Virtues to Modern Values*. New York: Vintage Books, 1996.

Chapter 1:
The Need for Character Education

Barton, Paul E., Richard J. Coley and Harold Weglinsky. Order in the Classroom: Violence, Discipline and Student Achievement. Educational Testing Service, 1998.

Confucius. *The Analects*. Oxford: Oxford University Press, 1993.

Covey, Stephen R. *The 7 Habits of Highly Effective People: Restoring the Character Ethic*. New York: Simon and Schuster, 1989.

Dhammapada. In *The Wisdom of Buddhism*. Christmas Humphreys. New York: Random House, 1961, pp. 45-52.

Etzioni, Amitai. *The New Golden Rule: Community and Morality in a New Democratic Society*. Basic Books, 1998.

_____. *The Spirit of Community: The Reinvention of American Society*. Touchstone Books, 1994.

Josephson, Michael. The six pillars of character. *Ethics: Easier Said Than Done* 19 & 20 (1992): 65-81.

Kilpatrick, William. *Why Johnny Can't Tell Right from Wrong*. New York: Simon and Schuster, 1992.

Lickona, Thomas. *Educating for Character: How Our Schools Can Teach Respect and Responsibility*. New York: Bantam Books, 1991.

McClellan, B. Edward. *Schools and the Shaping of Character: Moral Education in America, 1607-Present.* Bloomington, Ind.: Educational Resources Information Center, 1992.

McGuffey, William H. *Fifth Eclectic Reader.* New York: American Book Company, 1920.

Oliner, Samuel, and Pearl Oliner. *The Altruistic Personality: Rescuers of Jews in Nazi Europe.* New York: The Free Press, 1988.

Ryan, Kevin. Promoting responsibility in the classroom. *Character Newsletter* 1, No. 3 (April, 1993): 4.

Scotter, Richard D., John D. Haas, Richard J. Kraft, and James C. Schott. *Social Foundations of Education,* 3rd ed. Englewood Cliffs, N.J.: Prentice Hall, 1991.

Senge, Peter M. *The Fifth Discipline: The Art and Practice of Learning Organization.* New York: Doubleday, 1990.

Swartz, Robert. Teaching moral reasoning in the standard curriculum. In *Learning for Life: Moral Education Theory and Practice.* Edited by Andrew Garrod. Westport, Conn.:Praeger, 1992, pp. 107-130.

Wynne, Edward A., and Kevin Ryan. *Reclaiming Our Schools: A Handbook on Teaching Character, Academics, and Discipline.* New York: Merrill Press, 1993.

Chapter 2:
Teaching for Character Development

Aristotle. Nichomachean Ethics. In *Readings in Western Civilization,* 4th ed., edited by George H. Knoles and Rixford K. Snyder. Philadelphia and New York: J.B. Lippincott, 1968.

Bloom, Allan. *The Closing of the American Mind.* New York: Simon and Schuster, 1987.

Damon, William. *Greater Expectations: Overcoming the Culture of Indulgence in our Homes and Schools.* New York: Free Press, 1995.

Delattre, Edwin J. Diversity, ethics and education in America. *Ethics: Easier Said Than Done* 19 & 20 (1992): 49-52.

Hester, Joseph P., and Philip Vincent. *Philosophy for Young Thinkers*, 2nd ed. Monroe, N.Y.: Trillium Press, 1987.

Kilpatrick, William. *Why Johnny Can't Tell Right from Wrong*. New York: Simon and Schuster, 1992.

Kohlberg, Lawrence. *Essays on Moral Development, Vol. 1, The Philosophy of Moral Development*. New York: Harper & Row, 1981.

———. *Essays on Moral Development, Vol. 2, The Psychology of Moral Development*. New York: Harper & Row, 1984.

Kurtines, William M., and Jacob L. Gewirtz, eds. *Handbook for Moral Behavior and Development, Vol. 3: Application*. Hillsdale, N.J.: L. Erlbaum, 1991.

Leming, James. Curricular effectiveness in moral/values education: A review of research. *Journal of Moral Education* 9 & 10 (1981): 147-164.

Lewis, C.S. *The Abolition of Man: or, Reflections on Education with Special Reference to Teaching English in Upper Forms of School*. New York: Macmillan, 1947.

Lockwood, A. The effects of values clarification and moral development curricula on school-aged subjects: A critical review of recent research. *Review of Educational Research* 48 (1978):325-364.

McNamee, S. Moral behavior, moral development, and motivation. *Journal of Moral Education* 7 (1978):27-31.

Milgram, S. Behavioral study of obedience. *Journal of Abnormal and Social Psychology* 67 (1963): 371-378.

Oliner, Samuel, and Pearl Oliner. *The Altruistic Personality: Rescuers of Jews in Nazi Europe*. New York: The Free Press, 1988.

Piaget, Jean. *The Moral Judgment of the Child*. New York: Free Press, 1965.

Plato. Crito. In *The Collected Dialogues of Plato*, edited by Edith Hamilton and Huntington Cairns. New York: Pantheon Books, 1961.

Raths, Louis, Merrill Harmin, and Sidney B. Simon. *Values and Teaching: Working with Values in the Classroom.* Columbus, Ohio: C.E. Merrill Publishing Co., 1966.

Rawls, John. *A Theory of Justice.* Cambridge, Mass.: Harvard University Press, 1971.

Rest, James R. *Moral Development: Advances in Research and Theory.* New York: Praeger, 1986.

Ryan, Kevin, and Karen Bohlin. *Building Character in Schools: Practical Ways to Bring Moral Instruction to Life.* San Francisco: Jossey-Bass, 1999.

Simon, Sidney, Leland W. Howe, and Howard Kirschenbaum. *Values Clarification: A Handbook of Practical Strategies for Teachers and Students.* New York: Hart, 1972.

Sommers, Christina Hoff. Ethics without virtue means no ethics at all. *Ethics: Easier Said Than Done* 19 & 20 (1992): 60-62.

Stewart, John S. Clarifying values clarification: A critique. *Phi Delta Kappan* 56, No. 10 (June, 1975): 684-688.

Taylor, Charles. *The Ethics of Authenticity.* Cambridge, Mass.: Harvard University Press, 1991.

Vincent, Philip. The teaching of ethics as a means to facilitate moral development in gifted adolescents. Ed.D. dissertation, North Carolina State University, Raleigh, N.C., 1991.

Chapter 3:
Achieving Civility in Schools:
The Merit of Rules and Procedures

Barton, Paul E., Richard J. Coley and Harold Weglinsky. "Order in the Classroom: Violence, Discipline and Student Achievement." Educational Testing Service, 1998.

Curry, Nancy E., and Carl N. Johnson. *Beyond Self-Esteem: Developing a Genuine Sense of Human Value.* Washington D.C.: National Association for the Education of Young Children, 1990.

Gossen, Diane Chelsom. *Restitution: Restructuring School Discipline.* Chapel Hill, N.C.: New View Publications, 1992.

Kauffman, James, and Harold Burbach. On creating a climate of classroom civility. *Phi Delta Kappan* 79, No. 4 (Dec., 1997): 320-325.

Montessori Children's House of Newton. Duplicated information, 1993.

Rauhauser, Bill. *The Planning Book for Implementing Effective Schools.* Lewisville, Tex.: Rauhauser Publications, 1993.

Stevenson, Chris. *Teaching Ten- to Fourteen-Year-Olds.* New York: Longman Publishing, 1992.

Sweeney, Jim. *Tips for Improving School Climate.* Arlington, Va.: American Association for School Administrators, 1988.

Vincent, Philip F. *Rules & Procedures for Character Education: A First Step Toward School Civility.* Chapel Hill, N.C.: Character Development Group, 1998.

Wilson, James Q. *The Moral Sense.* New York: Free Press, 1993.

Wong, Harry, and Rosemary Wong. *The First Days of School.* Sunnyvale, Calif.: Harry Wong Publications, 1991.

Wynne, Edward A., and Kevin Ryan. *Reclaiming Our Schools: A Handbook on Teaching Character, Academics, and Discipline.* New York: Merrill Press, 1993.

Chapter 4:
Cooperative Learning

Baxter-Yoder, Denise. Personal correspondence, 1993.

Developmental Studies Center. *Blueprints for a Collaborative Classroom.* Oakland, 1997.

Johnson, D.W., and R.T. Johnson. Social skills for successful group work. *Educational Leadership* 47, No. 4 (Dec. 1989/Jan. 1990): 29-33.

Kagan, Spencer. *Cooperative Learning*. Capistrano, Calif.: Resources for Teachers, Inc., 1992.

Kagan, S., G.L. Zahn, K. Widaman, J. Schwarzwald, and G. Tyrell. Classroom structural bias: Impact of cooperative and competitive classroom structures on cooperative and competitive individuals and groups. In *Learning to Cooperate, Cooperating to Learn*, edited by R. Slavin, S. Sharan, S. Kagan, R. Hertz-Lazarowitz, C. Webb, and R. Schmuck. New York: Plenum, 1985.

Kohn, Alfie. Caring Kids: The role of the schools. *Phi Delta Kappan* 72, No. 7 (March 1991): 496-506.

Madden, N.A., and R.E. Slavin. Mainstreaming students with mild academic handicaps: Academic and social outcomes. *Review of Educational Research* 53 (1983): 519-569.

Slavin, Robert. When does cooperative learning increase student achievement? *Psychological Bulletin* 94 (1983): 429-445.

_____. Research on cooperative learning: Consensus and controversy. *Educational Leadership* 47, No. 4 (Dec. 1989/Jan. 1990): 52-54.

Vessels, Gordon G. *Character and Community Development: A School Planning and Teacher Training Handbook*. Westport, Conn.: Praeger, 1998.

Chapter 5:
Teaching for Thinking

Adler, Mortimer, J. *The Paideia Program*. NY: MacMillan Publishing Co., 1984.

Ennis, Robert. A Concept of Critical Thinking. *Harvard Educational Review* 32, No. 1 (1962): 87-111.

Hester, Joseph P. *Teaching for Thinking*. Durham, N.C.: Carolina Academic Press, 1994.

_____. *Thinking and Reasoning for Character Development: A Teacher Notebook*. Claremont, N.C.: Hester Learning Press, 1995.

Chapter 6:
Reading for Character

Book of Wisdom (no author). Sisters, Ore.: Multnomah Press, 1997.

Center for Learning. *Creating a Values-Based Reading Program.* Rocky River, Ohio: Center for Learning Press, 1993.

Great Books Foundation. Choosing the Great Books Selections: Four Basic Criteria. Chicago: Great Books Foundation, 1992.

Hinton, S.E. *The Outsiders.* New York: Viking Press, 1967.

Kilpatrick, William, Gregory and Suzanne Wolfe. *Books That Build Character; A Guide to Teaching Your Child Moral Values Through Stories.* New York: Simon and Schuster, 1994.

King, Jr., Martin Luther. Letter from Birmingham City Jail. In *A Testament of Hope: The Essential Writings of Martin Luther King, Jr.,* edited by James M. Washington. San Francisco: HarperCollins, 1991, pp. 289-302.

Sommers, Christina Hoff. Ethics without virtue means no ethics at all. *Ethics: Easier Said Than Done* 19 & 20 (1992): 60-62.

Wynne, Edward A., and Kevin Ryan. *Reclaiming Our Schools: A Handbook on Teaching Character, Academics, and Discipline.* New York: Merrill Press, 1993.

Chapter 7:
Service Learning

Arnold, John. *Visions of Teaching and Learning: Eighty Exemplary Middle Level Projects.* Columbus, Ohio: National Middle School Association, 1990.

_____. A curriculum to empower young adolescents. *Midpoints: Occasional Papers of the National Middle School Association* 4, No. 1 (1993):1-11.

Bolton, Bruce. Their Best Selves: Building Character Education and Service Learning Together in the Lives of Young People. Washington, D.C.: Council of Chief State School Officers, 1997.

Conrad, D., and D. Hedin. High School Community Service: A Review of Research and Programs. Washington, D.C.: National Center on Effective Secondary Schools, U.S. Department of Education, Office of Educational Reserach and Improvement; and Madison, Wis.: Wisconsin Center for Education Research, School of Education, University of Wisconsin, 1989.

Kinsley, Carol W., and Kate McPherson, eds. *Enriching the Curriculum Through Service Learning.* Alexandria, Va.: Association for Supervision and Curriculum Development, 1995.

Kozol, Jonathan. *Children of the Revolution: A Yankee Teacher in the Cuban Schools.* New York: Delacorte Press, 1978.

Lickona, Thomas. *Educating for Character.* New York: Bantam Press, 1991.

Parsons, Cynthia. *Service Learning from A-Z.* Chester, Vt.: Vermont Schoolhouse Press, 1991.

Service Learning and Character Education: Report from Wingspread. Camden, Maine: Institute for Global Ethics, April 25-28, 1996.

Service learning graph from James Toole and Pamela Toole, Co-Directors, Compass Institute, St. Paul, Minn.

Sprinthall, Norman. Social role taking: A neglected method of promoting moral and ego development. In *Moral Reasoning in the Professions: The Interface Between Applied Ethics and Social Science*, edited by James Rest. Hillsdale, N.J.: L. Erlbaum, 199.

Chapter 8:
Moving to Implementation

DeRoche, Edward F., and Mary Williams. *Educating Hearts and Minds: A Comprehensive Character Education Framework.* Thousand Oaks, Calif.: Corwin Press, Inc., 1998.

Hoffman, Judy, and Anne Lee. *Character Education Workbook for School Boards, Administrators & Community Leaders.* Chapel Hill, N.C.: Character Development Group, 1997.

Huffman, Henry. Character education without turmoil. *Educational Leadership* 51, No. 3 (Nov. 1993): 67-71.

LeGette, Helen R. *Parents, Kids & Character: 21 Strategies to Help Your Children Develop Good Character.* Chapel Hill, N.C.: Character Development Press, 1999.

Leming, James. In search of effective character education. *Educational Leadership* 51, No. 3 (Nov. 1993): 63-71.

Urban, Hal. *Life's Greatest Lessons: 20 Things I Want My Kids to Know.* Redwood City, Calif.: Great Lessons Press, 1997.

MORE GREAT RESOURCES

Title

Title	Quantity	Price	Total
ADVISOR/ADVISEE CHARACTER EDUCATION 24 Lessons to Develop Character in Students, SARAH SADLOW		$24.95	
CHARACTER EDUCATION Superintendent's & Administrator's Guide To…, DUANE HODGIN		$3.95	
CHARACTER EDUCATION WORKBOOK A "How-To" Manual for School Boards, Administrators & Community Leaders, JUDITH HOFFMAN & ANNE LEE		$12.00	
DEVELOPING CHARACTER IN STUDENTS, Second Edition A Primer for Teachers, Parents & Communities, PHILIP VINCENT		$19.95	
JOURNEYS IN EDUCATION LEADERSHIP Lessons From Eighteen Principals of the Year, ALICE HART		$12.00	
LESSONS FROM THE ROCKING CHAIR Timeless Stories For Teaching Character, DEB BROWN		$8.95	
PARENTS, KIDS & CHARACTER 21 Strategies for Helping Your Children Develop Good Character, HELEN LEGETTE		$15.95	
PROMISING PRACTICES IN CHARACTER EDUCATION Nine Success Stories from Across the Country, MULTIPLE		$12.00	
PROMISING PRACTICES IN CHARACTER EDUCATION, VOL. 2 12 New Success Stories from Across the Country, MULTIPLE		$14.00	
RULES AND PROCEDURES The First Step Toward School Civility, PHILIP VINCENT		$14.00	
RULES AND PROCEDURES VIDEO The First Step Toward School Civility, 44. MIN, PHILIP VINCENT		$99.95	
TEACHING CHARACTER Teacher's Idea Book, ANNE DOTSON & KAREN WISONT		$24.00	
Parent's Idea Book, ANNE DOTSON & KAREN WISONT		$12.00	

SHIPPING:
Up to $25 .... $4
$25 to $100 .... $6
Over $100 .... 6%

Subtotal ___

NC Tax (6%) ___

Shipping Total ___

Form of payment: Check ☐ PO #___ Total ___

Make checks payable to:
Character Development Publishing, PO Box 9211, Chapel Hill, NC 27515-9211

Ship To:

Name — — — — — — — — — — — — — — — — — —

Organization — — — — — — — — — Title — — — — —

Address — — — — — — — — — — — — — — — — —

City: ___ State: ___ Zip: ___

Phone: ( ) ___ Signature: ___

FAX ORDERS: (919) 967-2139

For further information, or to schedule a Character Development Workshop,
call **(919) 967-2110**, or e-mail to **Respect96@aol.com** or visit our WebSite
at **charactereducation.com** (Call for quantity discounts) DC299

CHARACTER DEVELOPMENT GROUP
PO Box 9211
Chapel Hill, NC 27515

CHARACTER DEVELOPMENT GROUP offers complete resources,
including publications and staff development training for
the planning, implementation and assessment of
an effective character education program in schools and
school systems.